Poetry in Motion

GW00507975

Devon & Cornwall
Edited by Kelly Oliver

 Young**Writers**

First published in Great Britain in 2004 by:
Young Writers
Remus House
Coltsfoot Drive
Peterborough
PE2 9JX
Telephone: 01733 890066
Website: www.youngwriters.co.uk

All Rights Reserved

© Copyright Contributors 2004

SB ISBN 1 84460 369 5

Foreword

This year, the Young Writers' 'Poetry In Motion' competition proudly presents a showcase of the best poetic talent selected from over 40,000 up-and-coming writers nationwide.

Young Writers was established in 1991 to promote the reading and writing of poetry within schools and to the youth of today. Our books nurture and inspire confidence in the ability of young writers and provide a snapshot of poems written in schools and at home by budding poets of the future.

The thought effort, imagination and hard work put into each poem impressed us all and the task of selecting poems was a difficult but nevertheless enjoyable experience.

We hope you are as pleased as we are with the final selection and that you and your family continue to be entertained with *Poetry In Motion Devon & Cornwall* for many years to come.

Contents

Sarah Jennings (16)   41
Kirsty Hamilton (14)   42
Jonathan Norman (14)   43
Toby Hackford (14)   44
Hannah Barker (14)   44
Alice Turner (14)   45
Samantha Cockburn (14)   45
Jenny Mallett (13)   46
Sally Biddlecombe (14)   47
Rebekah Ash (11)   47
Elizabeth Evans (13)   48
Jacqui Holleran (11)   48
Athena Clements (13)   49
Kristabel Henry (13)   50
Sophie Percival (13)   51
Sally Edwards (13)   52
Philip Watson (13)   53
Michelle Smith (12)   54
Miranda Gent (12)   55
Ben Kingscott (12)   56
Amy Stapleton (11)   56
Roseanne Bromell (12)   57
Georgia Flynn-Hurley (11)   58
Neil Addington (11)   58
Robert Tucker (11)   59
Harriet Mitchell (11)   60

Grenville College, Bideford

Luke Bailey (13)   60
Eleanor Briggs (12)   61
Amber Kenshole (13)   61
Jas Kalsi (13)   62
Chloë Gibson (11)   62
Richard Bassett (13)   63
Gemma Donovan (14)   63
Elizabeth Hemmerle (13)   64
James Manners (13)   65
Joanna Williams (13)   66
Sam Mead (13)   66
April Braund (13)   67
Joshua Braddick (11)   67

Jessica Teuchmann (13)	68
Francesca Tomalin (13)	69
Ravisha Patel (13)	70
Emily Parkes (13)	70
Elizabeth Jury (13)	71
Emily Hyam (13)	72
Ali Taft (13)	73
Sorrel Nixon (11)	73
Laura Appleton (12)	74
Sarah Hookway (11)	74
Mark Harding (12)	75
Nicolle Hockin (11)	75
Joshua Taylor (12)	76
Mark Murgelas (12)	76
Danielle Johns (13)	77
Samuel Smith (12)	78
Ashleigh Clayton (11)	78
George Hockridge (12)	79
Verity Langham (12)	80
Alice Bevan (13)	81
George Morris (11)	81
Charlotte Nash (12)	82
Rebecca Ferguson (12)	83
Jack Smith (11)	83
Melissa Taylor (12)	84
Dominic Chave-Cox (14)	85
Jessica Oke (11)	85
Hannah Standford (13)	86
Rosanna Jury (11)	87

Ivybridge Community College, Ivybridge

Eleanor Birkett (12)	87
Amy Carter (12)	88
Sally Osborne (13)	89
Charlotte Littlewood (11)	89
Amelia Stitson (14)	90
Kelly Steel (13)	91
Jemma Flower (14)	91
Francesca McCarthy (11)	92
Tara Rendle (13)	93
Thomas Gilbert (12)	94

Rachel Bagshaw (13)   95

Mounts Bay School, Penzance
Edward Waters (13)   95
Charlotte Brown (13)   96
Emma Mace (12)   96
Jade Simpson (12)   97
Megan Frew (12)   97
Alistair Brown (12)   98
Zoë Worledge (12)   98
Lois McGaffighan (12)   99
Tom Wilson (12)   100
Corey Howes (12)   100
Christian Orchard (12)   101
Tamsyn Astley (11)   101
Lydia Ralph (11)   102
Marion Bennetts (14)   102
Charlotte Brown (14)   103
David Waters (14)   103
Amanda Adams (13)   104
Bethan Jones (12)   104
Trev Dugdale (12)   105
Ross Nicholls (13)   105
Amber Jones (15)   106
Charlotte Matthews (11)   106
Rebekah Tonkin (16)   107
Rebecca McGarry (15)   107
Peter Lower (11)   108
Torrian James (11)   108
Amy Hutton (11)   109
Emily Barnes (11)   109
Darren Keast (15)   110
Alisha Hollow (11)   110
Neil Blackmore (15)   111
Joe Shelton (15)   111
Jess Draper (11)   112
Cara Beeley (16)   112
Adam Williams (13)   113
Georgina Brockman (15)   113
Stephanie Shapland (15)   114
Jessica Gray (15)   114

Jennifer Anne Greenslade (11)   139
Jordy Glasson (11)   140
Rebecca Sedgeman (11)   140
Holly Stevens (11)   141
Chris Burt (12)   141
Alex Jones (11)   142

Poltair Community School & Sports College, St Austell
Vikki Rostock (13)   142
Emma Griffin (13)   143
David Neville (12)   144
Ben Douglas (12)   144
Scott Wiley (12)   145
Leah Emerson (12)   146
Chantel Bishop (12)   147
Aaron Crocker (13)   147
Natalie Henderson (13)   148
Rachel Olsen (12)   148
Matthew May (12)   149
Ben Rowse (12)   149
Melissa Lobb (12)   150
Peter Megarry (13)   150
Hannah Pink (13)   151
Bethany Chard (13)   151
Jess Ball (12)   152
Sara McFeat (14)   153
Joe Parkinson (13)   154
Laura Jago (13)   154
Laura Mathews (13)   155
Jess Mitchell (13)   156
Jonathan Keast (13)   156
Matthew Bale (13)   157
Shaun Collings (13)   158
Rebecca Pascoe (13)   158
Lucy Cornelius (13)   159
Claire Sowden (14)   159
Tom Richardson (14)   160
Alison Sturtridge (13)   161
Ben Robinson (13)   161
Andrew Phillimore (13)   162
Aleisha Page (14)   162

Nicholas James Parr (11)	187
Heidi Masters (12)	188
Rosie Wilson (11)	188
Joshua Nel (11)	189
Katie Ford (12)	190
Bryony Walker (11)	191
Jade Gardiner (11)	191
Louise Haley (11)	192
Joe Higman (12)	192
Sophie Bonney (11)	193
Talei Lakeland (16)	194
Abigail Whiteman (12)	195
Peter Churchill (12)	195
Holly Julian (12)	196
Tom Bray (12)	196
Sam Hicks (13)	197
Kaci Rickard (12)	198
Luke Best (12)	198
Rachel Dowrick (13)	199
Sam Armstrong (12)	199
Sarah Masters (14)	200
Charles Camps (13)	200
Verity Walker (13)	201
Yasmin Sweet (13)	202
Kelly Buscombe (13)	202
Emily Ratcliff (14)	203
Lauren Blazier (11)	204
Luke Payne (13)	204
Megan O'Connell (13)	205
Jade Bradley (12)	205
Andora Perkins (13)	206
Hannah Nel (14)	207
Joseph Green (13)	208
David Blount (13)	208
Emma Thomas (13)	209
Ella West (13)	210
Ysella Wood (13)	211
Kirsty Kent (13)	212
Lauren Beard (12)	212
Michaela Dyer (13)	213
Bobbie Musgrave (13)	213
Jasmin Hicks (13)	214

The Poems

Shadowed And Torn

Every day there's a fake smile worn,
Even though you feel shadowed and torn,
Behind those eyes hides envy and shame,
Under that skin is something to blame,
You look at everybody hiding your face,
Scared that someone might follow grace,
Running away from things to come,
Walking away from what you've become.

Rachael May Balsdon (14)

Minerva's Handmaiden

(Dedicated to a mentor and tormentor J R)

Changed from childhood to strange youth,
Entered I world's ways blind, uncouth,
Yet callow arrogance, soon brought low,
Allowing love's frail flower to grow.

A handmaiden of lady wisdom, Minerva,
Enclosed me within her amphorus hold,
To love with such sweet fervour,
A love as pure as gold,
As I surveyed her wondrous face,
Of guile shot and fine of grace,
My soul became her temple fair,
Became her my soul lacking care,
Blessed was the handmaid of Minerva.

Christopher Villiers (14)
Braunton School & Community College, Braunton

I Love It In Winter

I love it in winter
When the icy cold wind howls outside
And I'm warm and cosy inside!
I sit by the frost-covered window,
Sipping at hot cocoa
Staring out on to a blanket of white.
I stroll across the beach
Munching hot chips,
Whilst the bitter wind lashes out at my face.
I build men out of snow
And dress them up,
Dreaming that they awaken from their slumber.
I join children playing in the streets
Screaming when a ball of white hits their faces,
Leaving red marks of coldness.
Christmas comes,
Presents and gifts are given
And what Christmas really means is forgotten.
The family united,
All jolly and merry,
Wishing everyone peace and goodness.
Soon it won't be winter and a new year will begin,
Some say look forward not back
But I'll remember winter.
I love it in winter
When the icy cold wind howls outside
And I'm warm and cosy inside!

Rebekah Lucas (13)
Braunton School & Community College, Braunton

Beauty

The pearly-white ribbon
That swings through the dark,
Through the musty brown mess
So bare, so stark.

The rusty red ribbon
That curls around the white
So bold, so brazen
Not curled up in fright.

The charcoal-black ribbon
Thrown into the night
Merged into the grey,
An arc at its height.

The washed violet ribbon
That twists around the black,
Submerged in the darkness
Sent to the back.

And the coarse golden ribbon
The height of them all
Cuts through the dark,
Never to fall.

Briony Beckett (13)
Braunton School & Community College, Braunton

Above Me

I look up in the sky at night,
I see the brightly glowing moon,
Tiny dots light up the black blanket above me,
To think there are planets beyond Earth,
This universe holds many wonders.

Emma Foulds (13)
Braunton School & Community College, Braunton

Ancient Egypt

The Nile flows across the land.
The pyramids, gleaming white.
The Sphinx's body stretched across the sand.
River temples that glow in the sun.

Pharaohs. Their royalty spreads throughout Egypt.
Mummified when they die to be remembered forever.
Then they are buried in their pyramids,
Along with treasures which are lost for the rest of time.

Now the splendour of Egypt is crumbling away.
The pyramids. No longer white.
Shadows seem to grow and grow
And where majestic temples once stood.
Nothing is there to be found!

Shaun Carter (11)
Braunton School & Community College, Braunton

The Murderer

I roamed around
In the dead of night,
Silent, no sound,
Dark, no light.

Who was the victim?
I had no cares,
I broke in the house,
Crept up the stairs.

. . . But that was years ago,
Life is Hell,
Time goes slow
When you're in a cell.

Lucy Baker (14)
Braunton School & Community College, Braunton

The Fall Of Angarion

Lord Angarion, the white knight of old,
His sword arm long, his countenance bold,
All clad in white and silver and gold,
To battle he rode, to battle he rode.

Elf friend, troll slayer, protector of man,
Hundreds of enemies died at his hand,
Shining as the sun, saviour of the land,
To battle he ran, to battle he ran.

Around him stood his companions five
To find the false god and take his life,
That was the objective to which they did strive,
Onwards they pushed to Lunasquall's Hive.

Atop the sorcerer's tower our hero died,
A golden light burst from his wounded side
And from it Lunasquall could not hide,
To challenge the one god he had tried
And failed, his power ever denied.

Nicolas Copson (15)
Braunton School & Community College, Braunton

007

J umping, diving and dodging evil,
A mazing stunts to match,
M iss Moneypenny helps him out,
E xciting fights to come out tops,
S nazzy kit especially for him.

B eyond belief he never dies,
O n the ball and looking fine,
N umber one for fighting criminals,
D o you know who it is? James Bond of course.

Jessie Woodward (11)
Braunton School & Community College, Braunton

The Bombs Fell

We crept forward,
Silent as the stars above,
We waited,
No alarms came,
We crept forward again,
Then I saw it on the skyline,
The bombs fell.

We ran for the love of our country,
We threw all we had into that attack,
Many gave their lives,
I did not,
My sergeant lay dying as he spoke to me,
'God called to me before I fell,'
And then he was gone.

I made my way back,
Among the rotting bodies,
All my thoughts were with my daughter,
She was but three years,
Her curly blonde hair,
Her bright blue eyes,
My wife's cheery face,
Stolen from me,
Forever.

I go back to the trenches,
To wallow in my sorrow,
For perhaps one more day.

Charlotte Shipley (13)
Braunton School & Community College, Braunton

The Unscary Monster

Do you know what that sound is
When you go to sleep at night?
It's that monster under the bed,
Filling you with fright.

You think he's going to hurt you,
But he's really not that bad.
He just wants to be out and about,
That would really make him glad.

Your friends tell you he's scary
And he's really, really mean,
But how do they know anything?
He's never even been seen.

He's escaped from many houses,
He goes in at night to keep warm.
The noises you hear are him snoring
And he's gone at the crack of dawn!

Michelle Severs (13)
Braunton School & Community College, Braunton

The Aztecs

Dawn breaks
The sun warms the blood-drenched rocks
Of the great temple
In a city in the Aztec empire.

Midday
And the screams of men
Lead to their death
Echoes in the air.
The priest raises his knife,
It swishes through the air
And blood gushes out.
His heart ripped from him
And a prayer made
All to please their bloodthirsty gods.

Night and another soul is gone.

Daniel Wathen (11)
Braunton School & Community College, Braunton

I See And Hear

I see and hear the ancestral curse.
I see and hear the absolute citizens cry.
I see and hear the bloodshed around.
I see and hear the jailbird bleed.
I see and hear the equaliser salvo gash.
I see and hear the mature shattered silence.
I see and hear the departing mortals bless.
I see and hear this acute monody.

Adam Smith (15)
Clyst Vale Community College, Exeter

Independent

We met in the usual circumstances
Across a crowded room.
We speak every day by phone or text,
Always feeling confident.
We see each other all the time,
Learning every little detail,
But how do we feel?

We have no strong emotions towards them,
Just satisfaction and enjoyment.
But they are so different towards us -
It's either complete immaturity -
Or they're completely besotted with us.
They make life more complicated than necessary.

Is it right to be wanting space,
Individual social lives?
Is it right to be different in so many ways
That it makes certain activities unbearable?
Is it right to be so far away from everyone
When you live so near?

Do we want this to continue?
We love everything about them,
But don't love them!
Should we give it more time?
We admire them and what they do,
But don't have admiration to be with them!
Should we give it more time?
We understand their meaning and language,
But we don't have a mutual understanding of life!

I need my independence!

Rachel Noakes (16)
Clyst Vale Community College, Exeter

What I Love . . .

What I love about sleep is the ability to dream
What I hate about dreams is the wake up of reality
What I love about keys is their power to lock out the undesired
What I hate about the undesired is their necessity
What I love about pattern is its flair of creativity
What I hate about creativity is its many complications
What I love about light is its vivid colours
What I have about colours is its judgmental qualities
What I love about truth is its hidden secrets
What I hate about secrets is the want to tell them
What I love about expressions is showing feeling
What I hate about feeling is its frequent exhibition
What I love about drugs is their qualification for medicine
What I hate about medicine is its purpose
What I love about films is their release
What I hate about release is its capture
What I love about power is its responsibilities
What I hate about responsibilities is the world in your hands
What I love about independence is its space
What I hate about space is its empty loneliness
What I love about music is the whirling of notes
What I hate about notes is their confinement to music
What I love about speech is its crafty explanation
What I hate about explanation is its consequences
What I love about brothers is their ever-growing knowledge
What I hate about knowledge is its acceptance of arrogance.

Sophie Herbert (15)
Clyst Vale Community College, Exeter

What Is?

What is the night?
It is the darkness of love.

What is the sky?
It is a mass of nothing.

What is jealousy?
It is a lesson to be learnt.

What is imprisonment?
It is one long pain.

What is a cloud?
It is an open space.

What is the future?
It is the time to party.

What is life?
It is forgetting the past.

Gemma Wannell (15)
Clyst Vale Community College, Exeter

Ways To Say Disease

Spreads faster than fire
yet you cannot see it.

Reminds us how important
life is.

Turns happiness
to denial.

Paints your sky to black.

The end is your freedom
of life.

Ryan Stuart (16)
Clyst Vale Community College, Exeter

Who Are You With?

Who are you with?
I am with my friends.
Who are you with?
I am with no one. I walk alone.
What are you going to do?
I am going to cook my dinner and take my dog for a walk.
What are you going to do?
I am going to melt away in the evening sunlight.
Why are you doing that?
To look for happiness in the stars.
Would you rather be somewhere else?
No. I have a house here.
Would you rather be somewhere else?
My soul longs to be where I cannot go.
Do you need me?
No. I have got my dog.
Do you need me?
If only I knew.
Shall I come with you?
Yes. I need a companion.
Do you need a companion.
Yes. I need you!

Chloe Smith (15)
Clyst Vale Community College, Exeter

African Dance

I can see the cultural style that welcomes the spirits,
I can see the masks that hide the dancers,
I can see the worshippers, who become possessed by Shango,
I can see the spiritual communication that relates to rites of passage,
I can see the historian who prays for fertility,
I can see the Gum Boot dance of the mineworkers forbidden
                                        to play music,
I can see the children who are in awe of the storyteller,
I can see the dance, the African dance.

Kate Thomas (15)
Clyst Vale Community College, Exeter

Who Are You?

Who are you?
I am a girl with long hair and a clear head.
Who are you?
I have never found out. The world spins too fast.
How did you get here?
I came with my family from across the sea.
How did you get here?
Through a daze and a dream. I am not really here.
What are you doing?
I am dancing through life with a smile on my face.
What are you doing?
I am trying to stay alive.
What do you wish for?
I wish I was you. I long to be you.
Why do you need me?
You need me as much as I need you.
Why do you need me?
Because there is no one else.
Is love real?
I hope so. I think I am still in love.
Is love real?
Perhaps, but love has never found me.
Where do you belong?
I belong here with everyone I love.
Do you belong here with everyone you love?
Yes, but who loves me?

Adela Boak (15)
Clyst Vale Community College, Exeter

Fear

Fear of shadows of the night.
Fear of age engulfing sight.
Fear of losing that best friend.
Fear of having a lonely end.
Fear of hearts being broken.
Fear of views being outspoken.
Fear of seeing those packed cases.
Fear of forgetting valuable faces.
Fear of God judging me.
Fear of never being free.
Fear of having too much time.
Fear of hearing the last clock chime.
Fear of thinking an evil thought.
Fear of catching or being caught.
Fear of Jesus on His cross.
Fear of God's wrath and His loss.
Fear of pain that's caused by Satan.
Fear of facing that temptation.
Fear of thoughts of suicide.
Fear of family mortified.
Fear of seven deadly sins.
Fear of losing or to win.
Fear of having a chosen fate.
Fear of love, turning to hate.
Fear of death, and of life.
Fear of Earth without strife.

Danielle Wynne (15)
Clyst Vale Community College, Exeter

With Your Finger

Dub me with your finger to superimpose my thoughts
Numb me with your finger to throw me into a void of ice
Tune me with your finger to make me thrive again
Taste me with your finger to see the cosmic truth
Colour me with your finger to make dull images vibrant
Mutilate me with your finger to silence unheard voices
Truncate me with your finger to shorten the story
Corrode me with your finger to denude my wrapper
Paste me with your finger to keep me still
Mock me with your finger to keep me detained
Educate me with your finger to treat my senses
Patch me with your finger to repair old times
Create me with your finger to make me true
Greet me with your finger to give me experience
Perceive me with your finger to unveil my secrets
Illustrate me with your finger to make me superior
Save me with your finger to make me hold on
Infect me with your finger to have evil thoughts
Devour me with your finger to make me drool
Clone me with your finger to witness my imperfections
Mute me with your finger to let me heed your word
Impede me with your finger to end this ode.

Lucy Poulson (15)
Clyst Vale Community College, Exeter

Love/Hate

What I love about friends is their caring smile.
What I hate about smiles is their patronising look.
What I love about speech is the freedom to express.
What I hate about freedom is that nobody cares.
What I love about beaches is the crashing waves.
What I hate about waves is their need to destroy.
What I love about music is the emotion it brings.
What I hate about emotions is their warrant to hurt.
What I love about books is the different worlds.
What I hate about the world is racism and segregation.
What I love about the oceans is their penetrating depths.
What I hate about depth is there is always more to find.
What I love about art is its refinement to galleries.
What I hate about galleries is the tranquil silence.
What I love about death is remembering good times.
What I hate about time is the eternal wait.
What I love about starlight is the twinkle in eyes.
What I hate about eyes is their edgeless stare.
What I love about hate is the passion and fear.
What I hate about love is the never-ending journey.

Danielle Sparks (15)
Clyst Vale Community College, Exeter

First Lesson

This is a meditation:
A dog with hands,
A handy dog,
A dog with horns,
A horny dog,
A hedgehog with spikes,
A killer hedgehog,
A hedgehog that listens to music,
A rocking hedgehog,
A snail that moves,
A marathon snail,
A snail that flies,
A super snail,
A fish without fins,
A dead fish,
A fish that runs,
The first round-the-world fish,
A tree that munches children,
An eating tree,
A tree that shrivels into a spider,
A spider that munches lots of children,
(You are not meditating).

Lizzy Anderson (15)
Clyst Vale Community College, Exeter

With Your Lips

Touch me with your lips to wake me up inside.
Calm me with your lips to fill me with blackness.
Sway me with your lips to clear my head of clouds.
Mortify me with your lips to give my eyes their reason.
Anger me with your lips to show the colour of my blood.
Relax me with your lips to silence my thoughts.
Mock me with your lips to feel my body transform to ice.
Control me with your lips to grant me answers I lack.
Deceive me with your lips to tingle the evil spirits.
Daze me with your lips to make it ethical once more.
Question me with your lips to perplex my soul.
Fluctuate me with your lips to discompose my understanding.
Caress me with your lips to mourn my heartbeat.
Kiss me with your lips to receive a warm sense of feeling.

Amy Peters (15)
Clyst Vale Community College, Exeter

Blind

Unpack me
Reveal me
I need to be spoken
I am a token
Eternal to the melancholic ache
Stroke the starlight
Stroke the stars
My tick-tock paintings
The oddity I created, fumbling
Bumbling
Nervous wreck
Predict me
I cannot see.

Tanya Southard (15)
Clyst Vale Community College, Exeter

Crowded

Crowded by the people
Of corporations and politics.

Crowded by the people
With pain of their own.

Crowded by the people
Doing anything to win.

Crowded by the people
Being forced to lose.

Crowded by the people
Who have more than they deserve.

Crowded by the people
Who deserve more.

Crowded by the people
Trapped by their greed.

Crowded by the people
Trapped by their need.

Crowded by the people
Who take from the world.

Crowded by the people
Who give what they don't have.

Crowded by the people
Living their life.

Crowded by the people
Struggling through greed.

Crowded by the people
Who want what I have.

Crowded by the people
Who need what I have.

Rudi Salisbury (15)
Clyst Vale Community College, Exeter

Music Is Freedom

Music is freedom
Freedom is life
Life is seeing
Seeing is believing
Believing is trusting
Trusting is friendship
Friendship is helping
Helping is donating
Donating is giving
Giving is losing
Losing is anger
Anger is hatred
Hatred is enemies
Enemies is war
War is killing
Killing is murder
Murder is prison
Prison is confinement
Confinement is rehabilitation
Rehabilitation is freedom
Freedom is music
Music is freedom.

Luke Davies (15)
Clyst Vale Community College, Exeter

Racism

R idicules and taunts in a child's eye always makes the child cry.
A nna is black and George is white, why do they always fight?
C hildren always grow up in pain, knowing that they've been
   put to shame.
I wish I could teach people the way, to love each other every day.
S kin colour does not matter to me, it's what's deep inside that
   I only see!
M ay you like me, just like I am, because you shouldn't judge me
   on my colour!

Megan Acton (12)
Cullompton Community College, Cullompton

Innocent

'Innocent!
That's what I am,
That's all I'm guilty of
Being innocent!
Being normal!
Now I'm trapped,
Trapped in me
Prisoner, for
Being normal!
Guilty till proven . . .
I'll never get out,
Trapped in nothingness for
Being innocent!
Being normal!
Stuck,
Forever.
What did I do, except for
Be normal?
Can you hear my cries?
Will anyone?
That's all I'm guilty of.
That's what I am,
Innocent!'

Oriana Clift (12)
Cullompton Community College, Cullompton

Racist

R is for rights which all of us have.
A is for armies which dominate their souls.
C is for civil which all of us need to be.
I is for insecure which people make them become.
S is for society in which we all do live.
T is for tomorrow when it will happen again.

Sarah Caller (13)
Cullompton Community College, Cullompton

Colours

C olours, people judge us before they know us.

O ver and over I live through the taunts wherever I go day and night, every second dreading to go outside.

L osers shouting, swearing and calling me names, it hurts inside.

O thers join in because the big shots call the shots.

U s, we are people not criminals, don't treat us differently, all we have done is be here.

R ainbow people, if I were yellow or purple or blue, would you still treat me as you do?

S top it, you've gone too far, you've won, now let me be, you've done enough damage for a lifetime.

Hannah Griffey (12)
Cullompton Community College, Cullompton

Racism

D ifferent skin colour can't be helped

I n different colours this might be so

F or each one needs love,

F or each one feels the same inside,

E ngland might be white, but there is no need to be racist,

R acism is not to be done,

E gypt might be black but don't be racist,

N ever will racism stop black and white bonding,

T alk to different coloured people because you might
                                         learn something.

Ashley Sinkins (12)
Cullompton Community College, Cullompton

Trapped

Trapped, trapped in a prison camp,
When I could be happy and free.
Digging holes in a hot desert island,
In so much pain I will be.

No water for miles, no towns you can see,
Can't run away, nowhere to go.
I'm all alone, no friends I have here,
Being picked on, they like making a show.

I miss my family so much,
Won't see them for years.
I must go home
Or I'll burst out in tears.

Jess Howe (12)
Cullompton Community College, Cullompton

Racism

R acism is a horrible disease that attacks the heart
   and can't be cured.
A person is a sensitive thing, at times it is strong,
   but racism still hurts.
C ure this and fight back, they are wrong not you.
 I don't judge people I love them for them for who they are.
S top this and find the cure.
M ake your life and build it up strong and remember you are
   beautiful no matter what anyone says.

Emily Couzens (12)
Cullompton Community College, Cullompton

Me

You don't know me,
You never will,
You can't see me,
I don't think I exist,
I don't think I ever will,
I can't see me either,
My mind isn't stable,
My hands don't work,
My life isn't real,
There's nothing left I can do,
They're always grieving, in anger,
Their hearts are almost empty,
What happens now?
What will it become?
What am I . . . ?
Dead!

Amy Wagstaff (12)
Cullompton Community College, Cullompton

I'm Not Different!

T hey think I'm different,
H e thinks I'm different,
E veryone thinks I'm different.

S ame as you, just a different colour,
A nd maybe from a different culture,
M any say that we're the same,
E veryone's different on the outside,
    but we're the same on the inside.

Natasha Smith (12)
Cullompton Community College, Cullompton

Different We Are Not

D ifferent are we, in no way at all,
I nside we are the same.
F eel the same, we do,
F ree are black and white people.
E arth is a place for all people,
R acism is bad,
E qual are we all,
N ever will racist people stop the black and white bonding.
T he same race, the human race, we are all in!

W illing to do whatever it takes to be accepted,
E ating with a hint of fear in their eyes.

A wakening into a world of hatred,
R acism is a thing that shouldn't happen,
E ffective and hurtful it is to them.

N o way am I going to just let this happen,
O utraged am I about this,
T ry and try will I to stop this.

James Parker (12)
Cullompton Community College, Cullompton

Racism

R acism is a horrible thing to do to people with different colour skin.
A person should be able to go without being laughed or pointed out.
C itizenship is what we need because people always need
                                        a helping hand.
I nstead of racism we should be able to get on and be friends.
S kin colour doesn't matter for a friend, it's how they act.
M arrying a different coloured skinned lady, it's the love that counts.

Matthew Reed (12)
Cullompton Community College, Cullompton

This Isn't Right

T his is wrong,
H urting people
I sn't right,
S houting and fighting is wrong,

I think this is wrong,
S top being cruel
N o matter what we are,
T he world is made for peace.

R acism
I sn't
G ood,
H unting down people,
T here's a better way to live!

Naomi Abrahams (12)
Cullompton Community College, Cullompton

A Poem To A Racist

S omeone is destroyed
A s you hurt them inside,
M ake them cry, do they
E xist in this life?

I s there a race that has
N o one different?
S omeone is being hurt
I nside,
D eeply destroyed, think what it
   would be like if you didn't
E xist in this life.

Becky Montague (12)
Cullompton Community College, Cullompton

She!

She will . . .
always work hard
in uni and school.
Even if it's not your birthday
she'll make you a card.

She will . . .
find out your secret
if you drop any hints,
but she'll keep it safe
like a caveman with flints.

She will . . .
move everything around
whether it wants to or not,
but it looks good in both places,
trouble is, she does it a lot!

She will . . .
keep everything clean,
sparkling and shiny,
she's the best one that's been,
she's my sis, the family queen.

Ed Carpenter (13)
Cullompton Community College, Cullompton

Individuality!

R acism is *wrong!*
A ccept people for who they are.
C olour, hair and looks.
 I ndividuality is important!
S ome people are different so don't hurt them!
M any people are different so . . .
                    Don't do it!

Amy Harrison (12)
Cullompton Community College, Cullompton

Me And My Mum On The Road
To Wimbledon Fame

Remember the time I told you I'd win Wimbledon,
I thought you'd just laugh
But you just said, 'I believe in you.'

Remember the time I'd told you I'd be rich from tennis,
I thought you'd tell me to choose a different career
But you just said, 'I believe in you.'

Remember the time I told you tennis was the only life for me,
I thought you'd be angry
But you just said, 'I believe in you.'

There were many times I would have given up,
Now I know it was worth it,
I've won Wimbledon
Because my mum said, 'I believe in you.'

Daniel Loftus (14)
Cullompton Community College, Cullompton

Colour

C an you believe in someone who's black
O r someone who's white?
L ife is full
O f people who are coloured.
U ses of believing in people of different races is hard.
R you a friend of someone who's black or someone who's white?

Keeley Farrant (12)
Cullompton Community College, Cullompton

The Electrician

We were working late
And then we had food on a plate.
We went to the electric box
And then my partner flicked the switch,
I told him not to.

We had fun working,
Too bad you were smirking.
We had some funny jobs in the past,
Too bad it was our last.

The last house that we worked at
You were drinking tea,
You walked down the carpet
And then flicked the switch.
You were bolted across the room,
I told you not to.

Luke Croad (13)
Cullompton Community College, Cullompton

The Black Stallion

The jet-black stallion rose high in the air,
Hooves thrashing through the still darkness.

His hooves came speeding towards the dry ground,
His heart was pounding, he was scared.

His muscles were tense, his coat drenched with sweat,
He rose again as a clap of thunder roared overhead.

He was a terrified wreck when he met the ground again,
The storm was over but the black stallion's terror wasn't!

Sarah Abrahams (12)
Cullompton Community College, Cullompton

Racism Hurts

R acism is horrid,
A person is left out,
C olour doesn't matter,
I t hurts people,
S top racism, once and for all,
M ake people feel good about themselves.

H elp people feel welcome,
U are the same as everyone else,
R acism is like a disease that can't be cured,
T elling people they are different is mean,
S ome people don't have a heart to care.

Samantha Quigley (12)
Cullompton Community College, Cullompton

Racism

D on't listen, you're not different,
O r don't be sad you're the same,
N o way are you different, inside you are the same,
T he same human race we are in.

L ook around, you're scared,
I n prison, in your own home,
S top them and fight back,
T otally unaware of what they're doing to you,
E nough to make you cry,
N o one there to even care.

Deanna Kitson (12)
Cullompton Community College, Cullompton

Racism

A ny two may look alike but,
N o one is the same.
T wo people can be different but,
I nside they're the same.

R idicule is wrong,
A nti-racism is the answer.
C ulture does not matter,
I t's inside that counts.
S ome people just don't see that, it's
M addening that fact.

Ashley Duzy (12)
Cullompton Community College, Cullompton

Racism

N o one to help,
O n my own,
T errified of meeting them.

F ear of life,
A ct big in front of them,
I n prison, in my own home,
R acism hurts.

Caitlin Jones (12)
Cullompton Community College, Cullompton

Racism

R acism hurts people,
A person dislikes another because they are different,
C atch the insulters,
I *t hurts people inside,*
S top racism it's bad,
M ake the insulters learn a lesson.

Dominic Carswell (12)
Cullompton Community College, Cullompton

Misunderstood

M y life
 I s
S o
U psetting
N o one cares. I get
D umped on
E very time. Everything is
R uined.
S ee, no one cares. Don't you believe me?
T he time clicks
O ver and
O ver so
D on't worry about my life.

Samantha Jones (14)
Cullompton Community College, Cullompton

Remember The Time

Remember the time I took my first steps?
You won't know, you weren't there.

Remember when I tied my shoe laces for the first time?
You won't know, you weren't there.

Remember the first day at secondary school? I was so nervous.
You won't know, you weren't there.

Where are you Dad?
You were never there.

Joanne Kelland (13)
Cullompton Community College, Cullompton

Misunderstood

M iss said, 'Do you need help?'
 I know I can do it
S o I try and try.
U nderstanding, that's what teachers do best, isn't it?
N ot a clever person me.
D on't do level 6 maths,
E ven numbers are double Dutch to me.
R emembering homework is hard too
S o I try - what's wrong with that?
T ests, tests, tests.
O n the front page it says, 'nice try'.
O f course I tried, but what's the point?
D on't ever get it right.

Lloyd Knight (13)
Cullompton Community College, Cullompton

The Real Me

T hink about me, what don't I need in class?
H elp, help is what I don't need.
E ven when I struggle, I don't need it.

R eally I am struggling,
E very day a new problem arises
A nd I cannot do it.
L ikely all alone, walking around.

M isunderstood, that's what I am,
E ventually you will understand.

Chris Finch (13)
Cullompton Community College, Cullompton

Being Born

For a long time
It was dark and warm and wet,
Then all of a sudden
I was out but where I don't know,
But then someone cut this long tube that gave me food.
Then all of a sudden I was crying
Because this midwife's hands touched me,
It felt like a cold winter's night.
Then this man with a green suit checked me all over,
It was really scary.
I got passed around like a present.
After this I saw my dad's face
And it was like he could never stop smiling.

Stacey Ward (13)
Cullompton Community College, Cullompton

Class Clown

C an you hear me
L oudly shouting, screaming for help?
A nswers are easy (not)!
S itting at the back of the class,
S tupidly.

C rying at home,
L onely,
O n my own, people don't listen,
W hy?
N obody likes me. Do you?

Daniel Matthews (13)
Cullompton Community College, Cullompton

My Name Is . . .?

My name is . . . ?
I don't know,
You see I have no friends to call me,
I thought I would but I don't,
Others wide berth me,
For me . . . not a care in the world,
Do you have friends?

My name is . . . ?
I don't know,
Yes I have a heart,
All empty and broken,
Yes others have a heart,
But full of hate,
Do you have love in your heart?

My name is . . . ?
I don't know,
Nobody to walk home with,
Whilst others walk on by with mates and girlfriends,
I'm like a Billy no mates,
I wish someone would be my friend,
Do you have friends?

My name is . . . ?
I did have a life once,
Till it got torn apart,
By all the people humiliating me,
Ruining my life,
Do you have a life?
A name for me would be lifeless.

Daniel Godfrey (13)
Cullompton Community College, Cullompton

The Bully

What does the bully think of after school?
Whose life he's made Hell.
Making fun of someone's pain.
Sitting down for dinner with nothing nice to say.
The boy at the back of the room,
Not listening, not learning,
Not trying.

What does the bully think after school?
Coming home to his room to tone his muscles,
Ready for his next victim like a bird of prey.
He's the one who needs help, do you?

Nick Carswell (13)
Cullompton Community College, Cullompton

Terrorist At Home

What does a terrorist feel when he sits at home
playing with his detonator?

What does he feel when he's running into a town centre
with a load of plastic strapped to his stomach?

What does he feel when he sees all
the people he is about to kill?

What does a terrorist feel?

Scott Struthers (13)
Cullompton Community College, Cullompton

I Am Who I Am

I am what I am, not what you want me to be.

A in't very good at spelling,
M any people say.

W ho are you?
H elp me please,
O pen a gateway to freedom please.

I am who I am, not what you want me to be.

A m I clever? No way I'm not, help,
M iss, please listen to me.

James Couzens (13)
Cullompton Community College, Cullompton

What Does A Soldier Think About At Home?

How can the soldier talk after his day?
How can he eat his dinner after all the shots he's fired?
How may he play with his children after all the near-death experiences?
How may he face reality with the choices he has to take each day?
How may he carry on with the ones he could not save?
Can someone trained to kill ever love?
I think not.

Ollie Darlison (13)
Cullompton Community College, Cullompton

I Don't

Do you have a best friend
Who says she is and then goes off with someone else,
Laughing and linking arms?
I don't.

That leaves you out and bosses you around?
Do you have friends that think the world of you?
I don't.

Have you ever been so upset about this?
Do your friends talk and laugh about you?
Do you have real friends?
I don't.

Judith Pike (13)
Cullompton Community College, Cullompton

Lust For You

I see the words arranged on the page,
It all seems foreign.
I know I wrote them and all about you.
Only one word I really do not understand
Love . . .
Your name's still on the tip of my tongue,
The word love still joined with it,
But still I know a simple lust.
A simple lust caused by you.
I have not heard your voice or felt your touch,
I don't know the next time I will hear you, feel you.
Still as the days go by it feels like eternity is unfolding upon me,
You're still the one I will long for,
You're still the one who I let get away.

Charlene George (15)
Dawlish Community College, Dawlish

Same Old Man

I wish that I could tell you just how it felt,
Sitting and watching the ice fade and melt,
Sat in the place that he always takes me,
The same old cafe, with the same old tea.

The same old smell, hasn't changed at all,
The same old picture, on that same old wall,
Colours still the same as when he was young,
The same distant records that U2 sung.

Nothing ever changes and neither does he,
Conversation the same, always will be,
He doesn't want to be here, I can tell,
He looks like a student, waiting for the bell.

Then the food comes out, it still looks the same,
The same old waitress, with the same old name,
The room is covered in flickering lights,
You look out the window, the same old sights.

Once conversation dies and fades away,
He takes the hint, it's time to pay.
The steady no ending drive home feels long,
The whole journey with one repeated song.
He drops me home, and says a quick goodbye,
He says he loves me, he tells one more lie.
Then he drives away as fast as he can,
I feel I don't know him, but he's still, my same old man.

Kayleigh Picken (15)
Dawlish Community College, Dawlish

The Storm

As the clouds begin to gather
The rain begins to fall.
As the wind rattles the shutters
The night blocks out the light.

As the torrents of rain come down,
Dancing on the rooftops,
I lie awake just listening
To the noise of the storm.

The sky is lit for a moment
As the lightning rips the air.
The thunder drowns out everything
Except the thoughts I feel.

The storm begins to quieten now,
The air begins to calm.
As dawn's first light brightens the sky,
All the storm's energy gone.

Alex Pirrie (15)
Edgehill College, Bideford

Poem On Ballet Dancers

The serene swan descends from the heavens,
Legs outstretched, wings poised,
A pregnant pause in mid-air.

A sea of tentacles reach up,
Hidden by a curtain of downy white,
One flick of her hand, and she is gliding gracefully across
the shimmering ice.

Waiting in the wings, we cygnets twitch,
Tapping pointed toes,
Smoothing ruffled feathers.

Opening my eyes, I hear a voice calling;
No more time for memorising,
The ballet begins.

Helen Watson (15)
Edgehill College, Bideford

Reach Out Your Hand

As a newborn baby cries
A starving child will die.
As wedding vows are spoken
A lover's heart is broken.

In a land where the rain will never come,
In a place where the people cannot be as one,
As drought strangles the land
Reach out your hand.

As waters tear away a home
And a partner is left alone.
Where innocent animals are slaughtered
And a mother loses her daughter.

When the last shot echoes through the valley,
Where the rich man squanders his money,
When a desperate crime is unseen,
You can change what has been.

Where the poor are rejected,
Where a disabled child is neglected,
When disease captures a relation,
When despair fills a nation.

In a place without hope, bring peace,
To a person without faith, bring love,
To the future generations, bring joy worth giving,
To a broken world of fear, bring a life worth living.

Sarah Jennings (16)
Edgehill College, Bideford

Daydreaming

As I walk, I let my mind wander,
I think about my life,
What has happened?
What is changing?
What is to come'?
Those I love - my family and friends.
Those who make me laugh,
Those who make me cry.
Places I have been,
Landscapes I have marvelled at,
Events which have changed me,
People who have shaped me.
Mistakes I have had to pay for,
Apologies I have had to say.
Decisions I have made,
Things I have committed to.
Incidents, some sad, some happy.
People I have said goodbye to,
Those I have gained.
Tears I have shed,
Things I dream of,
What I long to do with my life,
What I wish to happen,
Places I wish to go,
Things I wish to see,
Dreams I have,
Hopes I have.

And then, I am home,
My walk is over,
My life continues . . .

Kirsty Hamilton (14)
Edgehill College, Bideford

Identity

It walked in a circle, under a blackened night sky,
Not knowing where it was going; only wishing,
Wishing that it would find somewhere,
Just somewhere,
To call home!

I felt like it had strings, puppet strings,
That controlled it and its emotions.
But it managed to break free of this leash!
This mark of nothingness.
But it started to show some emotion,
A memory from its past
With a shred of happiness attached!

It knew no family,
It had no family,
But it knew what it wanted,
The only thing it wanted!
That was an identity, to call its own.

It had no name, no gender
Not even identifiable features,
But it now had feelings and emotions,
It even had a voice to call its own,
But it knew that this was not enough.

Not enough to have an identity!

Jonathan Norman (14)
Edgehill College, Bideford

As You Walk Into The Room

As you walk into the room
A silence fills your mind,
Everything's in slow motion
You don't know what you'll find.

You sit on your cold chair
Staring at the floor,
The time ticks by so slowly
As they close the door.

You have one opportunity
To show what you can do,
All those years of schoolwork
It's time for something new.

Your future's in your hands,
All your work is done.
It's time to face the world,
Let the times roll on.

Toby Hackford (14)
Edgehill College, Bideford

Photographs

Photos of old,
Photos of new,
Photos of me,
Photos of you.
Seeing them there,
Staring at me,
My past and present family.

Uncle Albert,
Auntie Maureen,
And look at that
Old Bertie yawning!
Here they're preserved
For evermore,
The greatest collection you ever saw!

Hannah Barker (14)
Edgehill College, Bideford

My Best Friend Bethan

My best friend Bethan,
Is the greatest friend ever,
She is always there to help us,
She will cheer you up when you're down.

She is good at sport and maths,
We share some of the interests,
Such as horses, dogs and maths,
We also disagree on things.

All friends argue, but we don't, much,
Bethan has a great sense of humour
And is always up for a laugh.

Her brown hair flows like a river,
She smiles like a Cheshire cat,
She is as mad as a March hare.

But all in all she is the best friend anyone could have!

Alice Turner (14)
Edgehill College, Bideford

A Midsummer Dream

'Back again,' I say as I walk up the misty pier,
Back again to my land of refuge, answer to my prayer.

Every single night I return to my bitter-sweet land,
Wondering when I'll be torn away.

I can't cope with vicious, ugly reality,
It's just too unfair as it frowns upon me.

Searching as the angry mist, my troubles surround me;
Then I see eyes sparkling like glitter, troubles are gone.

Rushing towards them with an urgency so clear,
One tender moment as we meet.

Then suddenly gone from my haven,
Flung back into the bullying reality.

Samantha Cockburn (14)
Edgehill College, Bideford

Dreams

You can jump off a cliff and survive,
Fly through the open sky,
You can walk on water,
Rule the world,
But to do all this you must dream it.

On Monday night I was the Queen,
Tuesday I was a flying horse,
Wednesday I met Tony Blair
And just last night I dreamt
Of a slide in my bathroom!

But not everything you dream is happy,
You can see some dreadful things,
Go through horrible adventures
And yet it feels so real,
Nightmares is what we call them.

I love to dream of things I want,
Like for Christmas or my birthday,
It brings me excitement
And then I feel happy,
It's funny what dreams can do.

Some dreams make me relaxed,
Others make me scared,
Some make me laugh
And most of all they make me think
Dreaming is another world.

And the most amazing bit
Is when you open your eyes,
As everything has disappeared,
New things to see
And back to the real world.

Jenny Mallett (13)
Edgehill College, Bideford

999 Here Comes An Ambulance

In the dizzy swirl
Of a blurry scene,
Through the helpless injured
Who toss and scream.

A saviour they hear
In a mist of lights,
With a siren roaring
In the dizzy heights.

A voice behind you,
A glint of green,
Someone helps you,
Paramedics at the scene.

A prick in your arm,
A twitch on your neck,
The ceiling of the ambulance
A swaying ship's deck.

Sally Biddlecombe (14)
Edgehill College, Bideford

The Worm

Amongst the grass and sandy dirt,
Between the muddied stone,
Across the roots of plants and flowers
A little worm makes his home.

He wriggles, he swiggles, he squirms about
Until at last the day is out.

He rests among the glossy willow
With the soft brown earth as his pillow.

Rebekah Ash (11)
Edgehill College, Bideford

Moving Schools

Silent mouthed I passed around my sweets
And drank in the classroom I wouldn't work in again.
All around me my friends chattered loudly,
Scribbling down their addresses on scraps of paper.
They would have to write to me now,
We couldn't just sit in a corner of the playground.

I packed my old work into my school bag,
Moving like a mechanical doll.
My best friend Hannah bent down to help me,
Until there was no trace of me left in the classroom.
On command we ran to leave for home;
For others this was a short holiday, but not for me.

With good luck wishes ringing in my ears
I walked across the playground I used to know,
As I turned to face the gate,
My friends encouraging smiles lingered in my mind;
They are sunshine on a rainy day.
Yes, I thought, *I am ready to start anew.*

Elizabeth Evans (13)
Edgehill College, Bideford

Moving

I love Devon so much so.
I moved from Rochdale to Devon
And the beach seemed like Heaven.
The sky was clear and bright blue,
The sea was calm and greeny-blue too
And so we stayed on the beach until seven.
As we left the beach I went into a dream
As I ate a massive, delicious ice cream.

Jacqui Holleran (11)
Edgehill College, Bideford

Ambulance Time

'Quick, over here . . .'
The men in red coats come running over . . .

'We were only playing,' I explain.
The men are too busy to listen,
I watch them as they hustle and bustle,
But this is no stranger,
This is my friend . . .

I look at the stream now,
The clear water turns a deathly red,
The liquid keeps on coming,
Coming, coming . . .

'We need to take her to the hospital.'
I knew this would happen, I solemnly nod my head.
Why, oh why couldn't I have just slept and stayed in bed . . .?

I watch as they take her away,
One hand droops over the stretcher,
As if waiting for me to follow . . .

Two weeks have passed,
And I often come to visit her,
She grows stronger every day but her memory is a distant thing.
One day I know her memory will return
And that day I cannot bear . . .

She will remember the argument we had,
She will remember us fighting
And then she will remember that I pushed her,
Pushed her, pushed her . . .

And over the cliff she fell, she fell . . .
She fell.

Athena Clements (13)
Edgehill College, Bideford

Bullied

Dreading the playground and after school times,
Walking down corridors, I'm next in line.
I am spat at and pushed, but do not cry,
I do everything wrong, I don't know why.

In French they throw chewing gum at my hair,
No one seems to notice or even care.
They tease and scribble all over my books,
They mimic my walk, make fun of my looks.

And just before lunch they take my money,
In their sick minds they think it is funny.
School hours get longer and longer each day,
They always taunt me and get their own way.

I try not to let my emotions show,
Try not to worry about tomorrow.
They say I can run, but I cannot hide.
Mum asked how I was, again I lied.
No one understands what's happening to me,
Except the bullies, but they cannot see.

Kristabel Henry (13)
Edgehill College, Bideford

The Salon

The hairdresser's is a very busy place,
With people sitting at every space,
Mirrored reflection face to face,
Some with wet hair, some with dry,
Some just coming for a try.

As the hairdresser snips and sheers,
Amazing styles start to appear.
Many people choosing highlights,
Reds, blues and shades of violets.
Spiky hair is all the fashion,
Gel and hairspray help this passion.

A bride is hoping for a surprise,
As she sits, her eyes are wide,
Will it be straightened, curled or coloured?
She watches as the styles unfurl;
Will it work? If it doesn't
She will go berserk.

People dying for a change
Will come in here to explain.
A layer here, a tint there,
The smell of perms pervades the air.
Different hair is on the floor,
You could make a wig or four.

Sophie Percival (13)
Edgehill College, Bideford

New Bridges

I'm building new bridges,
Building a new life.
It may take time,
But finally I'm free from your spite.

You made everything so hard,
Poisoned by your own hate.
I was easy enough to capture,
As one of them posed as a mate.

True, it wasn't all that bad,
You helped me to be free,
But looking back,
You just changed me.

You left me all alone,
So I returned home,
And made my greatest discovery
And that was me.

I've got over what you did now,
All the 'mates' you stole.
I watched every evil action, carefully plotted,
Yet the burden shall lie on your soul.

Sally Edwards (13)
Edgehill College, Bideford

Emotions

I'm pulled, dragged down,
I try to resist,
The murky depths grip holds tight,
I'm falling,
Water surrounds me,
My lungs fill,
My scream calls but is suppressed by a thousand tiny drops of liquid,
Limbs aching I struggle helplessly, please, please,
Fluid floods my body, I become numb,
Sucked below,
Gasping,
Pleading,
Begging.

I see again,
My senses alert,
Shaking, I reassure myself,
Sometimes emotions take over,
It was just the way I was feeling.

Philip Watson (13)
Edgehill College, Bideford

The Leopard

Concealed within dark, dense branches,
Listening intently for a sign.
Vivid orange eyes, wary of the scene,
Body tense, hungry, waiting to dine.

Razor-sharp swords prepared for a feast,
A peppered statue, like a frozen jigsaw,
Silently waiting for his prey.
A hapless jackal alert, senses raw.

She does not see the spotted creature,
Yet she knows danger is hovering.
Suddenly, the ground behind her beats,
Ferociously, the leopard is chasing.

Helpless, hopeless, desperately running,
Seeking shelter from the opposite side,
Fear and sweat saturate her frame,
Terrified, exhausted - she cannot hide!

Pitiless instinct drives him onwards,
Nothing can stop him - there are no laws,
With a heart of stone the leopard pounces
And swipes the prey between its jaws.

The leopard has had his feast,
A feast for him alone.
The battle is won. All is lost.

Michelle Smith (12)
Edgehill College, Bideford

Rubbers

People underestimate rubbers,
Really they're *extraordinary* things.
They come in all shapes and sizes,
But I've never seen one with wings.

A friend of mine had a rubber,
Thirty centimetres long.
It *was* quite thin,
But amazingly strong.

What I find annoying,
(I could almost have a fit)
Is when I need my rubber,
It's never where I put it.

Although you might not think it,
Rubbers come from a far away land.
Borneo is their origin
And is covered in forest, not sand.

If it hadn't been for my special rubber,
This poem would not have been right.
So keep them in mind, and always be kind,
To the friend of whatever you write.

Miranda Gent (12)
Edgehill College, Bideford

Retriever

I have a dog and he is a retriever,
He has teeth like a mountain beaver.
He eats all day; he's very fat,
I lis very boot friend is a tabby cat.

I pick him up, into my bag
Where he sits proudly with his rag.
He quietly chews it, ripping it up,
Making a noise like an angry wolf pup.

When we reach school, he has fun,
He doesn't learn much, he's very dumb,
But the teachers do not mind too much
Because he doesn't cause much trouble as such.

I come back home; he's tired like me,
So we settle down and have some tea.
It's silent, quiet, very still,
So I place him back on the window sill.

Ben Kingscott (12)
Edgehill College, Bideford

Winter

Winter is here every year,
It's coming, can you hear the cheers?
The snow has started, piles and piles,
Let's go out and walk for miles.
Crunch, crunch, crunch as I walk through the frost,
Very much hoping that I don't get lost.
Christmas is in wintertime,
Trees at Christmas smell of pine,
Sparkling of the lights as I sit down to dine
To my turkey and Brussels, pudding and pie.
Dressed at my best with Dad sporting his new tie,
Christmas has been great,
But now I have to wait
Until next year!

Amy Stapleton (11)
Edgehill College, Bideford

Words Worth Hearing

I once met a person who told me this,
You should think before you act, you know,
And smile before you kiss,
Your world is like a mass of mysteries,
You'll never know what's next to come,
But if you look a little deeper
You'll find the answer to the sum,
No matter what you do, no matter what you say,
You can never change the past,
So don't rush into things, there will be another day.
Also remember good comes with bad,
But that's just the way it is,
Don't let it make you sad,
For the good days will always win,
Just keep smiling,
Make sure you listen to the voice within.
This advice please remember for all of your days
Because the beginning will never begin again,
And the end won't give any clues away.

With this the person left me speechless on the spot,
I realised my life was not simple,
I would come across things I thought that I would not.
But like the person said that's just the way it is
With which I very much agree
And I now know,
That I am just as wise as he.

Roseanne Bromell (12)
Edgehill College, Bideford

Cleopatra

A cat that is slender,
A cat that is chic,
Cleopatra my cat is very sleek.
Cho'o black as the night
And silent as well,
Except when she runs
You'll hear her ting-ling bell.

She sleeps in the garden,
She'll sleep on a chair.
With her almond-green eye
Sometimes she'll stare
At the fish in the pond,
The birds in the trees.
Stealthily she creeps towards the leaves . . .
With a great pounce
The leaves start to fly.
We're the best of friends,
My cat and I.

Georgia Flynn-Hurley (11)
Edgehill College, Bideford

The Spider

The spider spends all day balancing on its web,
Still as a statue it waits and waits.
Hours pass
And just when the spider feels it is time to give up,

Suddenly a fly out of nowhere,
Not realising he will become an afternoon snack,
Flies into this deadly trap.

He desperately tries to escape,
The more he struggles, the more he is entangled in the sticky web.
He has one final attempt to break free
But his efforts are in vain,
As the spider moves in to collect his reward.

Neil Addington (11)
Edgehill College, Bideford

The Fight For Survival

Cold, wet and hungry
Sitting alone motionless
By a decrepit engraving on
An old iron bridge fishing
For hours on end.

Under the murky brown water
An eel was lurking alert
And poised to charge its prey.
There wasn't a ripple in the river,
Underneath the eel steaming towards a
Worm wriggling helplessly.
Snap!
It was all over.

The fisherman holding his rod,
Wound in his catch,
Thrusting
And
Twirling
And
Thrashing and smashing
The mighty eel broke free!

Robert Tucker (11)
Edgehill College, Bideford

There's Something Lurking At The Bottom Of The Village Pond

There's something lurking at the bottom of the village pond,
I don't know how it got there or whether it will stay for long!

The water that was once as clear blue as the sky
Has become dark and dreary.
Nobody stops to look anymore, they merely walk on by.

But I will change all of that.
I shall dive in and mooch around
And not leave until I have found
What lurks at the bottom of the pond!

People will be happy, people will cheer,
As they remember what a natural beauty they have right here.
No more will they just pass by,
They will stop, rest, picnic and play, from very early in the morning
Until late in the day.

And what was it at the bottom of the pond,
That tarnished the water and poisoned the fish?
Why it was all of our rubbish, that was the cause of all this!

Harriet Mitchell (11)
Edgehill College, Bideford

The Beach

The beach is such a great place to be!
Sitting in the sun and swimming in the sea.

You and your brother digging in the sand
With an ice cream in your hand!

You've built a sandcastle with your spade,
You're very happy with what you've made!

The tide is coming in, it's time to go.
The sun in the air makes the sky glow.

Luke Bailey (13)
Grenville College, Bideford

The Bubble

As I sat there with my brothers
A hoop plucked me from my room.
I watched as a strange world grew around me
And then a face began to show.

I watched the ground slowly disappear
As I floated into the air.
I began to spin as a breeze caught me
And I drifted helplessly.

I rose up high, then drifted down,
I thought I would come to land
But a current caught me and blew me up
Till it died and I fell back down.

I thought I might float forever
But I landed on a tree,
There I stayed for a little while
Before leaping off and flying dizzily.

I don't know when my journey will end,
Maybe I will fly forever
Or maybe I will find the place
Where a bubble is supposed to go.

Eleanor Briggs (12)
Grenville College, Bideford

The Swan

T he swan glides gracefully across the lake,
H er head held high and poised,
E ffortlessly she saunters.

S trong and loyal she is,
W ith her snow-white feathers,
A pair of beady eyes that twinkle
N oticing everything as she sways.

Amber Kenshole (13)
Grenville College, Bideford

A Different Day

Don't you wake up in the morning
Wondering what's going to happen today?
You're lying in a comfy bed
Where you just can't stay.

You're lying there still,
What's going to happen at work today?
You don't know for sure,
You're just wondering away.

Still thinking,
Still lying there with uncertainty.
You've got to think positive,
That nothing's going to hurt me.

All these different questions,
They need to have an answer.
Just look to the future,
You could become a dancer.

Your thinking needs to be over quick,
Because it won't be long
Until you finally realise
That the day has almost gone.

Jas Kalsi (13)
Grenville College, Bideford

Yellow

Yellow is like the red-hot sun which shines all day.
The warm heat of the sun.
The slow hot stars which take an hour to move.
Yellow is like the sandy beach near the deep blue sea.
The flying yellow bird.
The candle which dances in the wind.
Yellow feels warm and lovely.
On a sunny day people come out to play.

Chloë Gibson (11)
Grenville College, Bideford

Down Came The Rain

Down came the cold, wet rain,
Through the fields of golden grain.

The cool droplets, refreshing to touch,
Not many appreciate it much.
Questions arise to those who feel it first
And pleasant to plants to quench their thirst.

Down came the cold, wet rain,
Through the fields of golden grain.

A rumble of thunder, the skies grew dark,
A flash of lightning, just like a spark.
No more kids play in the park,
Cos down came the rain.

Through the fields of golden grain,
Down the river it so came.
A drizzle at first, then in torrents,
Down came the rain.

Richard Bassett (13)
Grenville College, Bideford

How Not To Write A Poem

I had to write a poem,
That's what my teacher said to me,
So I sat down upon my chair
And had a cup of tea!

Dolphins, drugs, school dinners (yuck),
I thought and thought of what to write,
It was all to no avail,
I had to stay up half the night!

Poems aren't my strong point,
I was worried, what my teacher would say,
But now I've almost finished, I've realised
That this poem must be handed in today!

Gemma Donovan (14)
Grenville College, Bideford

School

Monday morning, time to get up,
Bus will be waiting at seven.
Dash to the kitchen for cornflakes and milk,
Brush my hair, clean my teeth, good heavens!

I get on the bus, still half asleep,
Wanting to go back to bed.
Have I got everything I'm supposed to take?
I ought to check, that's what Mum said!

End of journey, here's my school
And there are all my friends.
Hannah, Emma, Stacey and Fran
And there's Liz in her Mercedes-Benz!

I've had my first lesson, second and third
And now it's time for break,
We sit together and have a chat,
But not for long or we'll be late!

The day is over,
The work is all done.
I've had a good day
And plenty of fun!
The bus is waiting to take me home,
I like school really, although I moan!

Elizabeth Hemmerle (13)
Grenville College, Bideford

Prison

I sit here in the dark,
Thinking,
Blinking,
It makes no difference.

What have I done?
Murder,
Killed her.
I sit in disbelief.

It's cold and damp,
Water drips,
Drips, drips.
No feel of warmth.

The bad boys all around,
Evilness,
Terrorists.
They fight from dawn to dusk.

The times are hard
Rough,
Stiff,
I might as well not exist.

I sit here in the dark,
Thinking,
Blinking,
It makes no difference.

James Manners (13)
Grenville College, Bideford

Don't You Wish?

Don't you wish you could turn back time?
Don't you wish you could see the people you love and never hate
Or could say sorry before it's too late?

Don't you wish you could turn back time?
Don't you wish that things were put right
And that you never had that last fight?

Don't you wish you could turn back time?
Don't you wish that you could have that last day together
Or say goodbye the way you wanted
And let them know you'll think of them forever?

Don't you wish you could turn back time?
Don't you wish you could?
You can't and that's the truth so think of them
The way that you should.

Joanna Williams (13)
Grenville College, Bideford

Autumn Leaves

The winter's calling,
Leaves are falling,
The snow white,
Much to children's delight.

The spring is near,
The brand new year,
But the lambs are early
The thick wool curly.

The summer upon us,
The swallow returns,
A pattern it has sussed
And always returns.

And back to the autumn
The golden leaves falling.

Sam Mead (13)
Grenville College, Bideford

Friends

I don't know what I would do without my friends,
They're always there for me,
They cheer me up when I am sad and always make me laugh,
They always look out for me,
I don't know what I would do without friends.

We always chat and make up jokes,
We normally watch films and go shopping,
But most of all they are there for me when I need them most,
My closest friends are Elizabeth, Gemma, Jess, Lizzy and Ravisha.

We always laugh, we always smile,
We normally sit next to each other in class and lunch,
We sometimes fall out but always make up,
We often write notes in class and normally giggle.

Friends are really important in life,
I can't imagine life without them,
I tell them secrets because I have their trust,
I will always smile when I remember my birthday parties with them.

They always stick up for you,
And normally share their break,
I will remember them even when I'm old and grey,
And all the good times we had together.

April Braund (13)
Grenville College, Bideford

Red

Red is the colour of roses
The sign of blood
The joyful movement of an excited cheetah
Red is the colour of a robin's belly
The flash of a killer
The screaming cheer of a devil's win
Red is the limitless expanse of fire below
The roar of a lion in the wood
Just before the morning comes I see red.

Joshua Braddick (11)
Grenville College, Bideford

An Early Morning Surf

I wake up early morning
The sun will slowly rise
The day begins here for me
It's the best surprise.

Into the car we hop and go
To arrive at my favourite place
Where to me my dreams come true each day
And where you meet the wave's true face.

The sand beneath my feet
The silence of the sun
The waves are the only noise
Each time is so much fun.

When the sun hits the waves
And the water sprinkles down
It shines as if it's glitter
The sea's no place to frown.

The breathtaking views
The cold but soft sea
The blue and green hues
Feeling happy and free.

Here comes the waves
Powerful, strong and fast
Carrying us into shore
I hope they last and last.

The feeling of standing, high on the board
Moving as if you're in the air
Although extreme, it feels so smooth
As if you've never had a care.

Now I've turned my back
On my best friend
I wish this glorious morning
Would never ever end.

Jessica Teuchmann (13)
Grenville College, Bideford

Space!

I open my eyes,
I don't know where I am.
Down beneath me,
Lies an unknown world.

I look all around me,
Stars whizz and whoosh around me.
Bang! A strange noise comes from behind,
I turn around in fear,
But what will I see?

Slowly I turn around,
Once again it's that strange sound.
An unearthly creature stood before me,
His face shone with glee.

Puffs of smoke came out of him.
He had come closer to me,
A strange parcel hangs off his limb,
He hands it to me.

I think to myself, shall I open it?
His face was still lit,
He can't hurt me,
So I opened it, bit by bit.
Whoosh! Out came a star and shot into the sky,
It was so beautiful tears came into my eye.

Francesca Tomalin (13)
Grenville College, Bideford

Fireworks!

As rockets shoot out fiery sparks,
And fall upon the sky.
Whizzing here and flying there,
As they fly up very high.

Catherine wheels spin round and round,
As fast as they can go.
Different colours at different times,
They make a fantastic show.

Roman candles are only one,
But don't shoot out so slow.
Bang! They go as they explode,
They make the night sky glow.

And in your hand you hold out far,
A sparkler is what you see.
A colour so bright, you hold so tight,
Writes names for you and me.

Ravisha Patel (13)
Grenville College, Bideford

Happiness

Happiness is a wonderful thing,
It makes you smile and makes you sing.
It comes up in different ways,
Lasting minutes, or sometimes days.

Whoever makes you smile, it could be a friend,
All the unhappiness, they seem to mend.
Whatever makes you smile, it could be a joke,
All the upset they seem to provoke.

You mainly get happiness with others,
Your friends, your family and even your brothers.
So remember it comes in different ways
Even on the worst of days.

Emily Parkes (13)
Grenville College, Bideford

The Wonders Of Space

When I look
On a clear, crisp night,
Awesome, amazing
A magical sight.

The sky cloaked in black velvet
With pin pricks of light,
Where a moth has made
A hole in the night.

The moon's golden smile
Beams down on the earth,
Perhaps our global warming
Is the source of its mirth.

Astronomy, beautiful,
Exciting, amazing . . .
But with more light pollution
The stars just keep fading.

People only care
About the things close around,
What about the wonders
In space to be found?

Elizabeth Jury (13)
Grenville College, Bideford

We're Nothing

100 lives we know nothing about,
100 deaths happening each day,
100 people we will never know,
100 words we will never say.

In a street somewhere in a town,
A girl's uncle dies in his bed,
Across the street a man jumps for joy,
He and his wife will wed.

So many different lives we lead,
Pointless, insignificant and short,
Wasted years in retirement homes,
And at schools when we were taught.

We're not going to live forever,
We'll all die whether we're poor or rich,
In life's towering tapestry,
What are we if but a stitch?

Children in a playground scream,
Old people in a home sigh,
What's our point in this world?
We've all been put here to die.

One day your thread will run out,
When you're a child, an adult or in your teens,
In 1000 years no one will know you were there,
That's how much your life means.

So many people you'll never know,
Makes it seem your life doesn't mean a lot,
So while your thread is still being spun,
Hold on to what you've got.

Emily Hyam (13)
Grenville College, Bideford

Morning Dusk

In the jet-black street
The odd star shows.

As the sun tip rises
So do shadows.

Dim and dark, dark and dim
Pockets of light arise.

The yellow lamp posts
Look from all highs.

Dull pavements
Dull houses
Dull sky.

No stars now
Birds just cry.

Ali Taft (13)
Grenville College, Bideford

Dolphins!

D olphins swimming freely,
O n the ocean wave,
L iving with a life of happiness,
P eace is all they need and if they're
H ungry they will eat the fish
 I n the ocean with them,
N ot knowing the fishermen will catch them,
S wim, swim, swim . . . !

Sorrel Nixon (11)
Grenville College, Bideford

An Autumn Day

When you wake up on an autumn morning,
Don't you love the way the dew settles on the ground.

The way the sun rises with its red and yellow glow,
But it soon rises higher for the day to go on.

The way the mist settles on the spiders' webs,
Which everybody look at with amazement.

The way the leaves are scattered around but are soon disturbed,
By people going to school or work.

The way everybody comes home from work or school,
And it gets dark by six o'clock.

The way you can smell all the sweet cooking
And seeing people going out to get takeaways.

The way all the lights get switched on or off,
With people going to bed, or watching television.

Don't you love all the autumn days!

Laura Appleton (12)
Grenville College, Bideford

Blue

The singing of the waves
The excited blue tits that come out to play.
The whispering of the sky
The howling of the dark blue night
Blue ice on a slippery pond

Blue, blue, blue . . .

The lonely cry of the seal.
The jumping dolphins of the sea
The planet Pluto never cares
The life of the rich blue sea
Is blue everyone's favourite colour?

Blue, blue, blue . . .

Sarah Hookway (11)
Grenville College, Bideford

Farm Poem

Lots of animals live on a farm
Some live in a covered barn,
There are cows, geese and sheep
Also chickens and the chicks go *cheep.*

In the spring we have lambs
Who play around with the rams,
And eat the food that we put down
With people watching from the town.

We have a lazy animal, he's our cat,
All he does is sleep on the mat,
Frosty is his name
Sometimes he is a pain.

We also have a horse
Who runs around of course,
We have a dog whose name is Dan
The cows run away as fast as they can.

We have pheasants on our ground
They eat our corn and strut around,
Their squawk is like a noisy alarm
I like living on a farm.

Mark Harding (12)
Grenville College, Bideford

Red

Red is the sunset flowing over the sea,
Shining and bright, sparkling with glee.
The red rose opening, looking just right,
To start a new day, to finish the night.
Red is the wind all bustling and loud,
Also the stag so straight and proud.
The vixen running with all her might,
Away from the shadows, away from the night.
And as the night comes I drift off to bed
This is all I remember from the power of red.

Nicolle Hockin (11)
Grenville College, Bideford

My Team

Football is a brilliant game
It's fun and great to play
My favourite team is Liverpool
I watch them every Saturday.

My favourite player is Owen
So skilful and so proud
He's such a fantastic goal scorer
And loves to please the crowd.

Dudek is the goalie
Sometimes for him it's boring
When the opposition do not try
To get close with their scoring.

Anfield is their stadium
Their manager is Gerrard Houllier
It really would be a dream come true
If I could play there one day.

Joshua Taylor (12)
Grenville College, Bideford

Snow And Ice Poem

Snowflakes are falling
Blue as the sky
White as the snow,
Patterns are growing
And the winter is coming slowly.

When it is wintertime
I run up the street
And make the ice move
With my little feet
Crickle, crickle, crickle
Creet, creet, creet!

Mark Murgelas (12)
Grenville College, Bideford

Ref Rap

I show the card
I send them off
I blow the whistle
When I've had enough

Fans all chant
Supporters sing
Can't hear the word
I'd like to think.

He's brave
He's strong
His eyesight's great
He's not the man
We love to hate

He does no wrong
He's always right
He's on the ball
He's dynamite

It's plain to see
You must agree
The man to be
Is the referee.

Danielle Johns (13)
Grenville College, Bideford

Rugby

I love rugby, it's a great sport.
You chase an egg ball round a field
And jump over the line to score a try!
It's better than football, better than cricket
Who wouldn't like rugby?
The joy of scoring a try or even creating one is overwhelming.
If a try is scored a conversion takes place,
A huge kick by the fly half gains two more points!
Who wouldn't like getting caked in mud
And being crippled by a No. 8?
Well, girls might not, but they do still play rugby.
The satisfaction of hammering someone to the ground
With a huge tackle driving the opponent
Into the wet, muddy ground!
You should watch it on telly, it's great fun,
Especially when England are on!
I love rugby it's a great sport!

Samuel Smith (12)
Grenville College, Bideford

To The Moon On A Spoon

I once said to a wise old man,
'Why do you live with your head in a pan?'
'Ask me no questions, I'll tell you no lies!'
He said as it all began.

'I went to the moon on a silver spoon,
With my monkey and my cat,
When we landed I found to my surprise,
That the moon was horizontally flat!'

'Good job I brought some crackers!'
Said my monkey to my cat,
Then afternoon tea came upon us,
And that was the end of that!'

Ashleigh Clayton (11)
Grenville College, Bideford

Autumn

It was very hot
As soon as the weather changed
I froze on the spot
The animals started acting strange.

The fruit was ready
The apples were red
I picked them steady
Enough for every head.

The leaves turned brown
Then left the tree and floated away
And landed near a town
Where they had no say.

Everyone is leaving the sea
Going back to their home
It was meant to be
There was one big drone.

Autumn has passed
And every tree is bare
Time is scarce
Winter is here, it's now very cold.

George Hockridge (12)
Grenville College, Bideford

Classroom Horrors

Paper aeroplanes sweeping and swooshing
Paper balls being crunched
Things flying through the classroom
People running out tho way, in a rush

Loud shouting and crying
This is where someone gets hurt,
Friends run over, just because she's toppled over.

A kick on the shin
A punch on the nose
Now a boy has bulging toes.

Here comes the teacher
Tap, tap, tap on the ground
There the children sit just after they're bound.
Squeak, squeak, squeak, the teacher's round the corner.

Children sit in silence
Not a spot of dirt on the floor
And there are the children ready and waiting
For some more uproar.

Verity Langham (12)
Grenville College, Bideford

The Witch

You see her standing there,
Her cloak black like the dead of night,
The pointed hat upon her head,
The hair underneath, so straggly and greasy
Falling limply round her shoulders.
The slitted eyes with their stare so cruel,
The long hooked nose on her wrinkled face
And the thin lips curling.

You see her standing there,
And you try to hurry on by.
You dodge her cat with its sleek, glossy coat
And tell yourself you mustn't look round.
But you can't resist, a peek can't hurt,
You turn and see those bony hands,
A living skeleton reaching for something.
You look up at her face and into her eyes,
But now you have made your fatal mistake
For she has you in her spell forever.

Alice Bevan (13)
Grenville College, Bideford

Black

Black is the colour of suffering
Black is the colour of death
Black is not even a colour
Black is the opposite of colour
It is all that is terrible and scary
It is all that is wrong
Black is the master of night but not day
Black is the servant of the Devil
Black is a hazard
It is all that hurts you and the world
As we speak it is hurting someone
Driving them crazy.

George Morris (11)
Grenville College, Bideford

The Raging Storm

The sea is rising,
Higher and higher it goes.
Rushing around your legs
And through your toes.

The white foamy horses,
Gallop towards you.
You hear a whistling,
You don't know what to do.

The storm is closer,
But you're still here!
You think you have plenty of time,
But it's getting near.

You look up at the clouds,
They're heavy and black.
Giants in the sky,
You'd better get back.

Something hits your head.
A raindrop, hurry!
You won't get back in time,
You're starting to worry.

Starting to run,
It's a race against the clock.
Nearly there,
Just passing the dock.

Finally you're home,
Cosy and warm.
You look out of the window,
At the raging storm.

Charlotte Nash (12)
Grenville College, Bideford

Feathers Of An Owl

It watches people pass and hope its life is worth
All this pain and misery and why he was put on earth.

He wished he were a human to walk and not to fly,
Though people may all stare at him cos when he talks he cries.

When he spreads his wings and soars and hovers from on high,
Catches a mouse in his sight and plummets until his throat is dry.

He thinks you don't appreciate all the things he does for you,
Come to think of it, what does he do?
He kills mice for a living and calls out in the night
And keeps on calling out until the dawning of first light.

We wake and he is sleeping with his wings behind his back,
And perched up on his favourite branch like spices on a rack.

When we come he flees away not a sound made from his wings,
A high-pitched note comes towards you and you swear an angel sings.

The final thing that happens as he gently swims away,
Is the smile he gave to me before the first sun ray.

Rebecca Ferguson (12)
Grenville College, Bideford

Red

Red reminds me of my team
I know I am with it by my side
The moan of the crowd
The love of the hearts
The blood of the soul
When the world roars you know you are safe
In 3-4 minutes you are free
Maybe it could be destiny
Maybe it just could be a dream
But what I do know is if you keep red by your side
You will be safe because you will never be alone.

Jack Smith (11)
Grenville College, Bideford

Dear . . .?

I don't really have a clue,
Who you are and what you do.
It really doesn't bother me,
As I'm into writing as you can see.

My mum told me yesterday I'd meet someone bad!
Who'll make me ever so, ever so *mad*.
I've been like that since they amputated my nose.
'Cause I was attacked by a flock of crows.

I wondered where you live
In fact I wondered what you're called
I wondered what you look like
Perhaps you're fat and bald!

I know you're not that interested
But I'm sure it will come out,
If you want to know what I do all day,
I am a pro, for fishing, for trout!

I just wondered if you care,
'Cause I 'ave some trout to spare,
If you did want some, come to my house
Then if you're lucky you'll meet my pet mouse!

Melissa Taylor (12)
Grenville College, Bideford

The Silent Soul

There is no sound in this dark alley,
Save the squeaking of vermin.
This secluded zone is cordoned off,
By a barrier of feelings and emotions.

No joyful thoughts can save me now,
My morbid soul I lay to rest.
To rot amid the world's delusions,
A tearful grave of sorrowful blood.

I raise the shotgun to my head,
I will not see but they will hear.
For they will weep and they will mourn,
But they know not my deep sorrow.

My final seconds passing by,
I pause to think of when and why.
Then clasp my finger on the trigger,
Breathe long and deep . . . and fire.

Dominic Chave-Cox (14)
Grenville College, Bideford

The Ballerlong

'What's a Ballerlong Daddy?'
It's a ballerina stuck to some gum,
Not just any gum though my son,
But all green and goey,
And can fight kung-foey,
That's a Ballerlong my son.

So it's a ballerina stuck to some gum,
That's all green and goey,
And can fight kung-fuey?
Yes, that's a Ballerlong my son.'

Jessica Oke (11)
Grenville College, Bideford

A Title Says Too Much!

People think I'm big and clever,
People think I'm cool,
I destroy the lives of everyone,
So I'm not so cool at all.

I give them all a buzz,
But what they cannot see
Is deep, deep down I'm hurting them,
I don't care, it ain't me.

They take me to fit in sometimes,
But really they're falling out
Because what I do is destroy them,
But I'm not gonna shout.

I'm gonna mess their heads up,
Play around with every cell.
I'm gonna end up killing them,
I deserve to be in Hell.

So remember everybody,
Don't think of taking me
Because drugs aren't big and they're definitely not clever,
Without me you are free.

Hannah Standford (13)
Grenville College, Bideford

Shades Of Blue

Shimmering azure is the song of dolphins
Leaping through tropical turquoise seas;
The magnificence of a darting kingfisher as it streaks
Over the sparkling river and into cool overhanging trees.

An early evening sky speckled with the first gleaming stars,
The moist mistiness of the moors on a cold winter's day,
The cry of a tearful puppy trapped in a rusty cage,
The melancholy sadness of billowing smoke makes me think of
blue-grey.

Sapphire is the sparkling gleam in the eyes of a magical princess
Admired by a blue-blooded, dragon-slaying lover.
Blue is the colour of smelly French cheese
And blue is the air when they scream blue murder!

Bluebells dancing in the fresh spring breeze
A delicate carpet of indigo under a crisp cerulean clear sky.
Indigo is the colour of deep icy water in a secluded bay
And the graceful fluttering cobalt butterfly.

Rosanna Jury (11)
Grenville College, Bideford

Love

Four letters of endless power,
Strength in any language,
Ever blossoming, like a flower,
More healing than a bandage.
Though it can sometimes sting,
Though it can sometimes smart,
Love comes on a gentle wing,
Because love comes from the *heart*.

Eleanor Birkett (12)
Ivybridge Community College, Ivybridge

Unknown Places In Nature

The sun sets in a distant place,
Scared to show its powered face,
The sun sets and the moon appears,
Shadows creep out with no fears,
Embracing its surroundings, setting it free,
Into unknown territories for all to see.

The wind's voice calls out its name,
To follow a path shown by the rain,
Streams run through a distant land,
Their route is not known or planned,
Trees look at the stars above,
Like a picture for nature's love.

Creating a song for all to sing,
Of the hope and peace it might bring,
The sun rises, brightening the atmosphere,
Listening to the song only nature can hear,
The grass dances in a swaying motion,
The beautiful sky like a tranquil ocean.

Nature's sound is peace where the light goes,
This beautiful emotion that all of nature knows,
This form of music sounds night and day,
Showing in every single way,
No more tears of despair,
There is only hope for all to share.

Some dream of all there could be,
The boundaries they could see,
All the things they'd have to greet,
Some new songs they would meet,
However these are dreams of where they want to go,
These are all the places they want to know.

Amy Carter (12)
Ivybridge Community College, Ivybridge

Hands

A blind man's hands touch everywhere and everything.
They let his mind imagine, they let him see
The world, his world.

A baby's hands are gentle, soft and innocent,
Yet when they grip onto something,
They never let go.

An old person's hands are frail and wrinkly,
But look closer and they tell a tale,
A tale of happiness and sadness,
Their life well lived.

Look at your hands,
What do they say about you?

Sally Osborne (13)
Ivybridge Community College, Ivybridge

War

It was as cold as ice,
Scuttling over numb feet were mice.

It was as dark as night,
There was not even a flicker of light.

I heard screams, I heard wails,
I heard ripping, tearing, ferocious gales.

The great fear froze my brain,
The sound of many folk dying in pain.

Booms and blasts all around,
It was a terrifying painful sound.

Fire burst and flared above,
I longed, cried and prayed for Mother's love.

Charlotte Littlewood (11)
Ivybridge Community College, Ivybridge

Father Christmas

Heave, push, shove, wedge,
Grunt, poke, squash, prod,
His beard, normally long and white,
Was now an awfully terrible sight,
It hung from his chin in straggly locks,
His clothes dark and dirty, terrible frocks.
He bent down low with his bum in the air,
He didn't do it with grace, caution or care.
His trousers split open, a huge great gash,
His pants, a bright pink, were shown with a flash.
He hurriedly unpacked the parcels with care,
Presenting them all with majestical flair.
He stood with a clunk and entangled his hat
On the Christmas cards with a terrible *splat.*
He quivered, he tottered, he stumbled and fell,
Smashing into the Christmas tree, ringing the bell.
He tried to regain his balance and flee,
But instead he turned around and grabbed onto the tree.
He wobbled and fumbled and held on for dear life,
He thought of his reindeer, his children, his wife.
He slowly unwound himself from its branches,
Looked from side to side with terrified glances,
He heard voices and footsteps calling from upstairs,
He ran for the chimney, forgetting his cares.
As a last minute instinct, he grabbed for the food,
Gobbled down a mince pie, milk, to his reindeer he cooed,
'Rudolph, get them ready, I'm coming out any minute,
I need it ready so I can jump straight in it.'
He started to climb back up the flue,
Father Christmas had come, and left turmoil in this room.

Amelia Stitson (14)
Ivybridge Community College, Ivybridge

Alone

A boy in the snow,
He calls your name,
He bows his head,
A look of shame.

In his mind
He cannot see
A ray of hope,
Except for she.

She, whose face
Shows in his dreams,
But leaves him
Like the moonbeams.

A boy in the snow,
He does not call.
She did not come,
He did fall.

Kelly Steel (13)
Ivybridge Community College, Ivybridge

Scattered Daisies

Scattered daisies from that memory of you
Scattered daisies below the sky so blue.
As I lay beneath you I look to the skies
The starry twinkle in your eyes
Fields of our happy days
How I miss you in so many ways.
Always I know you are here
For you to leave again is my fear.
A ring of daisies like my feelings love borrows
Entwining around me, embracing my sorrows
My walls are caving in but you support me
Every move, every word you see
Scattered daisies I spread over you
I miss you so, I wish you knew.

Jemma Flower (14)
Ivybridge Community College, Ivybridge

A Brighter Tomorrow

Small, hungry children look up with tearful, sad eyes,
Everyone in the world seems to be telling them lies.
Their hope for the future is more or less gone,
But I am pleased to say that they could be wrong.

If you wish to help, you will succeed,
Creating for them a brighter tomorrow, that's what they need.
A little joy, a touch of happiness here and there,
They need someone to show that they care.

Help mend their sorrow and mend their broken hearts.
Happiness is what they need in small and big parts.
Make the sun shine brightly with your ongoing love,
And make them happy and peaceful just like a flying dove.

Helping and loving will make them smile.
Smiling is contagious, it goes on for more than a mile.
Wipe away their tears, put love in their life,
And bad things will away like grass with a scythe.

Creating a brighter tomorrow is what counts
Whether you do it in small or big amounts.

Francesca McCarthy (11)
Ivybridge Community College, Ivybridge

Card Games

An angel, a king, a rabbit and Death
Met in the park one day,
They played cards by the light of the angel's breath,
But never had one word to say.
The king hid the aces under his crown
As the rabbit ate the joker,
Death declared, with a frown,
That he much preferred to play poker.
At the ring of his voice, the rabbit froze,
The king took off his crown.
All the spirits around them rose,
And all the cards fell down.
The angel looked up to the sky
As the rabbit flew away,
The king took his leave to die,
But Death decided to stay.
An angel, a king, a rabbit and Death
Met in the park one day.
They played cards by the light of the angel's breath,
But only one stayed to play.

Tara Rendle (13)
Ivybridge Community College, Ivybridge

The Mistress Of The Night . . .

The mistress of the night . . .
Cold, unforgiving,
A cruelty to all that know her.
Sorrow oho brings,
Amongst many things
If your fear you dare to show her.

But she stands as a light,
In some people's hearts,
Aiding peace, rest and sleep.
She comforts the old,
She strengthens the bold,
And encourages those who are weak.

So there she would stand,
A two-sided band,
The traditional good versus evil.
And there she would wait
And watch for her fate,
Because when the sun comes up,
It's her turn to leave.

Thomas Gilbert (12)
Ivybridge Community College, Ivybridge

Slipping

Fragments of my broken heart
Could pierce through the eye of a needle,
Abandoned arms lay unwanted,
Bare in a room, being watched,
But feeling so alone.
Drowning in a pool of water,
Being pulled downwards,
Reaching out, trying to grab something,
Someone,
But it's gone.
Gasping for air,
A stampede of elephants have run over me,
Breaking me,
So I cannot feel happiness anymore.
A tear trickles down my innocent face,
Disappearing from my view,
Only leaving a distant memory,
From which a young mind grew.

Rachel Bagshaw (13)
Ivybridge Community College, Ivybridge

The Isles Of Scilly

Out towards Land's End,
You can see a place
Of calm and peace,
A place where miners will come
For pasties (home-made).

Old ladies will stop and stare
While having a cup of tea,
Boats will come from afar.

Ferries carrying old people's cars,
But now it's just me
And my old green car.

That's my Britain.

Edward Waters (13)
Mounts Bay School, Penzance

Britain

W e are an island on the sea,
E ating pasties, and ice cream with clotted cream.

L andmarks like Lanyon Quoit and Men-An-Tol,
O verlooking miles of blue-turquoise sea,
V eterans of the war
E ating from the great range of pubs and restaurants.

B eaches with golden sand and glistening blue waves,
R oses flying on flags as a symbol of Britain,
I ce cream melting down the cone in the hot weather,
T ennis players playing in the finals for our country,
A nthems playing,
I ce cream topped with Cornish clotted cream,
N ature, so full of it is Britain.

Charlotte Brown (13)
Mounts Bay School, Penzance

Beaches

Look at the turquoise water sparkling away,
The waves are soft and calm,
Washing themselves up on the beach.
The soft golden sand burns your feet,
Multicoloured seaweed spreads out on the beach.
It feels so slimy and slippery on your skin.
Little kids running around with ice creams in their hands,
Sandcastles and pictures decorated
With pretty little shells and rocks.

Emma Mace (12)
Mounts Bay School, Penzance

The London I Know

In the city of London
Comes an added rush of sound,
Where the children play, lovers walk hand in hand.

In the morning darkness silvers away,
The dusk disappears, then out comes the day.

As Big Ben sounds the first sign of morning,
The people get out of bed, still yawning.

The blankets of the deep blue sky
Arise to the city's fresh dawn.

The whisper of early morning sun,
Upon the roads it is for some.

Now on top of the Palace roof,
The blackbirds begin to sing,
As Big Ben sounds another ring.

Now the sky is spoilt as the factories start.
Stop the pollution, have a good heart.

Jade Simpson (12)
Mounts Bay School, Penzance

The Countryside

In the countryside you will see . . .
An angry, buzzing Mr Bee,
A squirrel running up a tree,
A little boy hurt his knee,
Couples having a cup of tea.
In the countryside you will hear
The pace of a fast running deer,
Horses shouting, are they near?
Cows charging, do you fear.
In the countryside you will smell
The fresh water from a well,
The metal clanging from a ringing bell,
The dirt from where a boy just fell.

Megan Frew (12)
Mounts Bay School, Penzance

Britain Is Great!

B ig Ben is a tourist attraction,
R angers and Celtic, the old firm rivalry,
I rritating, dreary winter weather,
T ony Blair, our Prime Minister,
A lton Towers, fun for all!
I mportant royal family,
N essie lives in Loch Ness.

I reland's capital, Dublin,
S cotland, not very good at footy, but a lovely place.

G lasgow, Scotland's city of culture,
R acing with Schumacher at Silverstone,
E lephants all around in London Zoo!
A irports at Heathrow and Gatwick,
T ower Bridge over the River Thames.

Alistair Brown (12)
Mounts Bay School, Penzance

Beaches

Bustling, with people swimming in the sea,
Each and every one of them putting on suncream.
Some people sit down to eat,
But they must beware of the seagulls.
They will ruin the feast.
Everybody trying to get the sand off their feet,
Knowing they will soon have to leave the beach.

Zoë Worledge (12)
Mounts Bay School, Penzance

Cornwall

Cornwall has got lots of space
Because it is a very big place.
There are lots of gorgeous beaches,
Where you can hear the seagulls' screeches.
Surfers are paddling in the sea,
While tourists have a cup of tea.
People camp out in the rain,
They think it is a real pain.
When the weather gets quite warm
For the night, there'll be no storm.
Little children build big sandcastles,
While their mothers straighten towels' tassles.
People lie on golden sand,
Using paper to get fanned.
If you look out on the sea,
You will probably have to see
The enormous St Michael's Mount,
And so many boats for you to count.
If you go out to a town,
You will hear lots of sounds.
If you want to be unclean,
Why not buy a big ice cream
Or a traditional Cornish pasty
Where the keeper isn't nasty.
This is Cornwall in my view,
Where the houses are not very new.

Lois McGaffighan (12)
Mounts Bay School, Penzance

Britain Is Fantastic

B ig Ben is an historic attraction,
R angers vs Celtic, the old firm derby,
I sles of Scilly, lots of little pieces of land,
T iuro is the capital of Cornwall,
A merica's David Blaine, a crazy man,
I n London's city centre there is the London Eye,
N orthern Ireland's capital is Belfast.

I pswich Football Club play in Division One,
S occer's the sport lots of people play.

F enland of Britain is flat and fertile,
A nfield, the home of Liverpool Football Club,
N ewcastle is near the city of Sunderland,
T aunton is where Somerset Cricket Club play,
A sylum seekers lurking in every town,
S nowdon, a famous mountain in Wales,
T ony Blair, the Prime Minister of England,
I ain Duncan Smith, the Tory party leader,
C athedrals in every city.

Tom Wilson (12)
Mounts Bay School, Penzance

Paul Scholes

P lays for England's first team,
A lways starts in central midfield,
U nless he gets injured,
L ovely little ginger.

S cores some smashing goals,
C areful in his tackles,
H e drives the ball forward,
O wen smashes it home,
L ots of goals he sets up,
E xcellent player he is.
S choles is my favourite player.

Corey Howes (12)
Mounts Bay School, Penzance

Great Britain Poem

Great Britain I've arrived at (such a small land)
Made up of England, Wales, Ireland and Scotland.
I'm going to England, best of them all,
I think I'll go first to the capital.
Next to see the famous Shakespeare's home,
Stratford-upon-Avon I will roam.
Onto the London Eye (oh, what a view),
Then the Millennium Dome, that's super too.
Off down to Cornwall, that's where I'm staying,
Instead of working, I will be playing.
The Cornish pasties, oh what a treat,
They just make you want to eat, eat, eat.
Wimbledon is really such a good place,
With tennis balls to hit right into space.
Cricket in GB is really superb,
When they hit the balls, some of them swerve.

Christian Orchard (12)
Mounts Bay School, Penzance

Great Britain

G reat Britain is lots of fun,
R etail therapy is number one,
E ven though we have lots of play,
A ll of us work hard most days,
T he food we eat, like roast dinners,

B uilds us with energy all day long,
R emember all the sports we play,
I n most events we take part,
T ennis, cricket, golf, football,
A re just a few things we do.
I n the sea, we splash around,
N ever get bored whilst on the beach,
    making sandcastles and burying our feet.

Tamsyn Astley (11)
Mounts Bay School, Penzance

My Favourite Cornish Food

I love to eat my Cornish pasties,
Sitting in the town centre
As I watch people walk past me.

I love to eat my Cornish clotted cream
And Cornish ice cream together,
Sitting on the beach as the waves tickle my feet.

I love to eat my Cornish cream teas
In a café overlooking the sea,
And I see a dolphin jump gracefully.

I love to eat my Cornish heavy cake with a glass of milk,
Sitting in the garden, and I smell cows
And I think how my milk got to me.

Lydia Ralph (11)
Mounts Bay School, Penzance

We Arrived On A Boat

In the morning we arrived on a boat
In the back streets of London.
Everyone looked at me and
Smiled to make me happy.
I knew we would like England
Because England is for everyone we see.
The British ways were new to me,
The British dancers were none to see.
When we arrived on that winter's day,
I knew that Britain was where I wanted to stay.

Marion Bennetts (14)
Mounts Bay School, Penzance

Britain

By day you can explore the Eden Project,
Tropical plants, animals and waterfalls.
It feels as though you're somewhere special,
Out of Britain, somewhere abroad.

By night you can watch a play
In the small village of Porthcurno,
Listen to the sea whisper,
And sit beneath the stars.

Another day you could visit a beach,
With soft sand and warm sea.
You could spend all day swimming
Under the sweltering sun.

Another night you could stroll along Penzance prom,
Lit by fairy lights all the way.
The crabs run up the wall
As you sit on a bench, watching the stars all twinkling.

Charlotte Brown (14)
Mounts Bay School, Penzance

Dartmoor

D ancing mist
A rt work in your eye
R obust views
T ors like mountains
M iles of countryside
O pen spaces
O blivious of anything else
R oaming cattle.

David Waters (14)
Mounts Bay School, Penzance

Fishing

Fighting for their lives, the fishermen of Cornwall,
In the rain and snow and storms.
Through night and day they strive away
For the welfare of their homes
As the fishermen relay and lower their nets,
They await the arrival
Of the lighthouse at its best.
The rusty, large, elderly boat
Sways into the harbour mouth,
As the buzz of the fish market
Echoes around the walls,
Awaiting tons and tons,
When the fish are frozen and packaged
And sent all over the world.
You cannot beat the wait,
Of the fresh Cornish taste,
From the fish and chips
We have brought you.

Amanda Adams (13)
Mounts Bay School, Penzance

Beaches

B ritain has a lot of beaches
E ach one has golden sand
A nd they all have cool blue sea
C an you stand the coldness?
H ats are on everyone's heads
E veryone's suncream goes on
S oon though, they'll have to go.

Bethan Jones (12)
Mounts Bay School, Penzance

Martin Johnson

M assive guy
A lways pushes his hardest in the scrum
R eally tall, 6'7"
T he captain of England 1st team since
I n the mid 90s
N ever missed a game for England

J uggles the rugby ball with ease
O n the pitch he stands out
H ot-shot in the rugby world
N ever drops a line-out
S o aggressive in the tackle
O ff the pitch he's so dedicated
N ot small, but huge.

Trev Dugdale (12)
Mounts Bay School, Penzance

Britain

It's like the big wheel at the fair,
Except there are millions of people there.
You can ride on it for half an hour
And see the London Tower.
It looks over the River Thames,
While you give others gems.
When it turns to night,
You can see London flooded with light.
Looking over London and seeing all those colours
Made my mother and brothers cry.
If there was any place to die,
It would be here, here on the London Eye.

Ross Nicholls (13)
Mounts Bay School, Penzance

Britain

Oh bonnie Scotland in the north
Has many things to be absorbed.
When it snows on a winter's day,
All the kids go out to play.

And then England, biggest of all,
From north of Newcastle to south of Cornwall.
So many things to be explored,
The London Eye is not to be ignored.

The emerald isle of the west
Has its four-leaved clover,
Which makes it luckier than the rest.

Then Wales, a land of countryside
Which is full of life and grace,
And on an autumn day, you can stand upon the beach
Watching the waves race.

This is why I'm proud to be British,
A land of nature and wildlife to see.
I would hate to go away, because I would miss it.

Amber Jones (15)
Mounts Bay School, Penzance

An English Roast

I love a traditional English roast,
My favourite is roast beef,
With crispy Yorkshire puddings
And crunchy roast potatoes,
With cauliflower and broccoli,
All heaped upon my plate.
My nice little carrot coins
And fresh garden peas,
All covered in hot gravy,
A proper Sunday roast.

Charlotte Matthews (11)
Mounts Bay School, Penzance

Britain

When I think of England,
The place that appeals to me
Is Cornwall for the pasties and the sea,
Surfing on the beaches and drinking Cornish tea.

Walking along beaches, admiring the sea,
Looking over the edge and wondering what's in it for me,
Surfers hitting the waves and trippers jumping with glee,
Eating Cornish cream teas, while seagulls are attacking me.

Walking through the countryside admiring the view,
Crossing fields and listening to cows go, *moo,*
Muddy wellies, waterproof coats and watching goats,
Admiring boats and looking at orange floats.

Friday comes and it's fish and chips for me,
Then out clubbing for a brilliant party.
Cornish mead, go to bed, get up in the morning with a sore head.
So that's my poem and now I'm going. See you in Cornwall!

Rebekah Tonkin (16)
Mounts Bay School, Penzance

Britain

B usy, bustling towns and cities,
R ushing people, tourists too,
I nteresting landmarks, places to visit,
T he Union Jack, the national flag,
A wide variety of race and culture,
I mmigrants, refugees live here too,
N umerous accents can be heard.

Rebecca McGarry (15)
Mounts Bay School, Penzance

Bad Weather

Bad weather affects us a lot in the UK,
Rain, surging floods,
'Raining cats and dogs',
Surging, surging,
Blowing out of gutters,
Splish, splash, splosh.
Rods of grey rain
Whipping ships in the sea as it goes,
Bursting banks,
Sand bags,
Weather forecast,
Blustery showers,
Drizzle,
Muddy ground,
Puddles,
And even if you're lucky,
The sun might peep through the clouds.

Peter Lower   (11)
Mounts Bay School, Penzance

The Cornish Coast

Underwater in the heat,
I feel the seaweed tickle my feet.
I swim around and try to find
A wave that I will dare to climb.
Then I see a dolphin leap,
And smoothly flow into the deep.
Then I laid there on the golden sand,
I began to feel like I was in another land.
Lying there made me roast,
That was my day by the Cornish coast.

Torrian James   (11)
Mounts Bay School, Penzance

Tower Of London

T orture chambers
O ld and ghostly
W hispering voices
E ndless shadows
R olling heads

O ngoing killing
F orever blood

L ives at risk
O n the rack
N o use complaining
D on't look back
O nwards is good
N ever give up.

Amy Hutton (11)
Mounts Bay School, Penzance

St Michael's Mount

There is a castle out at sea
We don't have to travel far to see,
It sits high above the rocks,
And underneath has little shops.
Many people like to travel along
The slip to see the castle.

There the flag flies high above,
The castle is a place I love.
You can walk there when the tide is out,
See all the people out and about.
When the tide is in, you go by boat,
Let's go, quick, get your coat.

Emily Barnes (11)
Mounts Bay School, Penzance

Britain

A few of the reasons Britain truly is great.
Look at the size of it, small, but so powerful,
Tiny but so strong.
The oak tree, our symbol stands proud.
The rose blooms to show Britain's beauty,
Unfolding in time.
Look at our long stretching beaches
And rolling coastlines.
Packed with ongoing life from our bustling cities,
Packed with ongoing life from our bustling
Fields and hedgerows.
Our livelihoods we make ourselves
Through farming and fishing,
So say it proud, because you know it's true,
Great Britain.

Darren Keast (15)
Mounts Bay School, Penzance

A Poem About Britain

F ish and chips
I ncredibly tasty
S alt and vinegar
H ave some more

A dd some flavour
N ice and hot
D on't feed the seagulls

C od, haddock, salmon, bass
H olidaymakers love them
I mpossible to leave
P opular St Ives
S upper delight.

Alisha Hollow (11)
Mounts Bay School, Penzance

England The Predominant

Separated lands
No longer combined,
England the predominant,
Strongly underlined.

England, Ireland, Scotland and Wales,
The flag of red and blue and white,
England the centrepiece of all its might.

The British bulldog combines us all,
With pride and victory
The patriots stand tall.

The biased don't brag,
Just make the most of what they have,
So the St George's Cross which implies the best,
Will continue as always to rise above the rest.

Neil Blackmore (15)
Mounts Bay School, Penzance

Britain

Britain, a land steeped in history
Kings, queens, princes, princesses,
Beheadings, coronations, births, deaths,
Old kings, young kings.

Old wars, new wars, family wars,
All in history,
War of the Roses,
First, Second World War,
Mad men trying to invade,
We conquered all.
Britain, a land steeped in history.

Joe Shelton (15)
Mounts Bay School, Penzance

The British Flag

Red, blue and white,
Are really quite a sight.
I really don't know why,
But the colours really f

                  l

                        y.

All day in the air
Would give me quite a scare.
They bring it   *d*
He gives a blissful frown.

                w

                n

Up on the flag pole
Fidgeting like a tadpole,
Up in the air,
Giving Britain a *f*   *y* stare.

              u   *n*

              n

Jess Draper (11)
Mounts Bay School, Penzance

My Poem On Britain

Britain smells of bacon and eggs and sausages and beans,
The full English breakfast, running down your jeans.
The English rose flowers again, with conkers and oak trees.
The Queen's mother is dead and the Queen is soon to follow.
The English bulldog symbolises Britain, just like the Queen.
And as for the Union Jack, that's famous
For flying on the palace as well as Geri's dress.

Cara Beeley (16)
Mounts Bay School, Penzance

What Am I?

When I was young my mum
Pushed me in a pram.
Now this is what I am.
I have a short fuse
When I'm accused.
Sometimes I still need a hug,
Because I get upsets and
I feel I'm going to blow up.
When I'm happy, I feel so good,
But when I run, I run with a hood.
No one knows me except for Nicky,
She's so understanding and not very thick.
When I argue, I feel so bad,
I'm sorry but they're still mad,
But when we make up, I'm glad.
People think I'm strong and never get sad,
No one knows me, I feel so bad.

Adam Williams (13)
Mounts Bay School, Penzance

Cornwall

Cornwall is at the end of England,
Some beaches covered with golden sand,
Attractions to holidaymakers,
Each one of them a leader,
It's full of the country and sea,
I really do think it holds the key,
But to find out, we'll have to wait,
Please tell me when you know the date.

Georgina Brockman (15)
Mounts Bay School, Penzance

Fields Of Gold

Poppies scattered, row on row, strewn across the fields of gold.
Each flower a remembrance of a life once lived and died
For the freedom of his country.

Mothers weeping, widows remembering the brave lions
Who fought to keep them safe.
The fatherless children left to remember a faceless name.

After the black tears have fallen upon grace on the lush lands
                                        of the dead
A new day of freedom will dawn, of bright sunlight glowing on the faces
Of those who lived to see the future of their country, they survived
By the fearless death of those beneath their feet.

When the sun sets and the sands of time pass the poppies
Scattered row on row, strewn across the fields of gold,
Shall forever grow and remember the souls
Who lived and died in the great wars.

Stephanie Shapland (15)
Mounts Bay School, Penzance

The Red Rose Of War

Overhead a million bombs tear by,
But still the soldiers stand.
For their country they are fighting,
The almighty lions.
For their country they are standing,
The strongest oak.
For their country they are dying,
The proud red rose.
For us they die a million deaths,
For our safety and our freedom.
For us they die a million deaths,
So we can live and be heard.
For us they fight until their dying day,
The heroes of our hearts.

Jessica Gray (15)
Mounts Bay School, Penzance

British Sunday

Waking to the sound of birds
Bells and choirs singing joyous words
Eggs and bacon, a wonderful feed
After having your Sunday read.

Preparing lunch for Sunday guests
Peeling veg,
So much for this day of rest.

Children's voices full of glee
Lying under duvets watching TV
All over Britain the doorbells ring
Sirloin for guests, knighted by a king.

After dessert, coffee or tea
Depart to the lounge
Watch Sunday TV.

When all the homework has been done
The evening pulls in
Down goes the sun.

Waking up
A hectic Monday
Dreaming of that British Sunday.

Edward Harvey (13)
Mounts Bay School, Penzance

The Magic Scoreline 5-1

When the scoreline was 5-1
England were the best,
A hat-trick from Owen,
A goal from Heskey
And Gerrard's goal was class.
So if ever England play Germany again,
I'll remember the magic scoreline 5-1.

Chez Jeffery (12)
Mounts Bay School, Penzance

Is Britain Really Great?

From John O'Groats to Land's End,
British soil covers the land.
Green, lush and surrounded by sea,
The British Isles are we.

From Vikings to Romans to present day,
Many have fought to rule this place.
From Robin Hood to Tony Blair,
Many men have led people there.

Loyal to our sovereign are we,
We celebrate Her Majesty.
With William rising to be king,
His mother, how we weep for thee.

From red phone boxes and cups of tea,
Cucumber sandwiches and roast beef,
Football hooligans, tennis flops,
But never a nation to ever stop.

We are a nation small in size,
Loyal, brave, but united we are.
Foreigners may mock and criticise too,
But British we are and will strive to improve.

Megan Hosking (15)
Mounts Bay School, Penzance

Commuting To Me?

C oming into work is for me?
O range zone and tickets please,
M essy trains with clapped out engines,
M issing bags and crying children,
U gly stations and interchanges,
T oo many people, too few seats,
I nto London at 9.03,
N othing but delays and cancellations,
G ood old British Rail!

David Tracz (13)
Mounts Bay School, Penzance

The Beach

The sea comes in and out again,
Over the rocks and sand.
People lie there all day long,
Trying to get tanned.

The surfers ride the waves up high,
The seagulls stealing chips,
As you look across the sea
There are lots of ships.

Children playing all day long,
Digging holes and bathing.
Lifeguards ready for a swim,
Diving in and saving.

When the sun goes down at evening
Barbecues are cooking,
Next year the camps will be full again,
With holidaymakers booking.

By September everyone's gone,
And shops are out of food.
Cornwall has much better beaches,
Especially at Bude.

Leanne Howarth (12)
Mounts Bay School, Penzance

Great Britain

Down here is the place to be,
For wonderful sights and scenery,
The only problem with Cornwall is,
The weather changes with a whiz,
Tourists fill in minute by minute,
To see Penzance and what is in it,
At Christmas Mousehole is the place to be,
For wonderful sights and scenery.

Samuel Gillaspy (13)
Mounts Bay School, Penzance

Britain

This island that we live on,
The greatest of the world.
The sea, the sky, the British air,
Is the value of this pearl.

We're the lions of this jungle,
We represent the brave.
Our legacy's depth
Goes beyond that of any cave.

The sweet scent of the red rose
Represents our island.
Its fragrance stretches
From Land's End to the brave Scottish Highlands.

Our weather's always different,
It never stays the same.
You could be set for beach weather,
The next thing you know, it's rain.

Our monuments are of plenty
From Stonehenge to Big Ben.
Our rugby team is second to none,
The greatest of British men.

Harry Bosworth (13)
Mounts Bay School, Penzance

Britain

B ig Ben is one of our most famous landmarks,
R oast beef is our nickname from the French,
I nto the pubs goes every race,
T ourists come from every country
A nd get attacked by fleets of seagulls,
I ce-cold winters with lots of rain,
N ow the tourists go home again.

James Blewett (13)
Mounts Bay School, Penzance

Britain, My Island

B ritain is my home, it's where I live,
R oast dinners on Sunday
I s a tradition we give
T he glittering sun in summer
A nd the cool sea breeze
I t's an island I love
N o other place would I be.

M y family's home
Y ou would never want to leave

I love all of its beaches
S urfing and swimming in the summer sea
L andscapes, countryside,
A nd cities and towns
N ight-time stars come out
D on't let the rain bring you down.

Becky Stains (14)
Mounts Bay School, Penzance

Great Britain

T he meadows are full of cows,
H ares darting without a sound,
E volution is accelerating.

B ritain is becoming a leader,
R eality is almost a dream,
I nternational business has become a routine,
T he world is now wiser,
A s is the modern eye,
I s this why new discoveries are not surprising?
N ow you must help to uncover Britain's true potential.

Ellis Hughes (13)
Mounts Bay School, Penzance

Britain

What does Britain mean to you?
To me, Britain is my home,
The island I was born on,
A place where I have lived all my life,
A small island,
With salty sea surrounding it.

To me, Britain is quite cold.
As I live in Cornwall,
I never know what to expect,
Rain or shine.
When it is warm and sunny,
The sea is cool and refreshing
And when it is wet and dull,
The sea is rough and dangerous.

To me, Britain is full of smells,
Sweet fudge, thick cream,
Cornish pasties,
Full English breakfasts in the morning,
Sunday lunch,
All different kinds of smells and tastes.

To me, Britain is a peaceful place,
Going on long countryside walks,
Walking along rocky paths,
Looking out to sea,
Being told many legends.
Britain is where I live
And that's what Britain
Means to me.

Vashti Maeckelberghe (13)
Mounts Bay School, Penzance

Britain

Great Britain is all about legends,
St Michael's Mount and more.

We are famous for our tin,
There are lots of mines around.

We live on an island,
Although we are quite big.
There are lots of people here,
In Great Britain.

We love our Cornish pasties,
And ice cream too,
We love to eat them all year round
And that's what we will do.

We are surrounded by sea,
Seagulls and fish too,
We have got a fishing business
In Penzance and Newlyn too.

Danielle Edwards (13)
Mounts Bay School, Penzance

Great Britain

I'm a full-blooded British stereotype,
Tea and biscuits,
Be polite,
Pale skin,
Strawberries and cream.

I'm a full-blooded British stereotype,
Cricket and football,
We made them up.

I'm a full-blooded British stereotype,
Not posh and not always start.

I'm a full-blooded British stereotype,
A human being just like *you*.

Jenna Barnett (13)
Mounts Bay School, Penzance

Britain In Union

England is white,
Scotland is blue,
The Welsh sport a dragon
For the RFU.
The venue down under
Will see the World's nations ply
Their skills and their muscle
To score every try.

When Dallaglio scrambles the ball
From the scrum,
He passes to Cohen who
Goes on the run.
He ducks and he dummies
And crosses the line,
And we all know that
Wilko converts every time!

Scotland valiantly took on Japan,
Who'll nip and tuck wherever they can.
Enough tries were scored,
To get bonus points,
But Scotland look like
They may have sore joints!

The Welsh dragons took on
The Maple Leaf Land
And showed us their mettle could
Clearly withstand
Whatever came at them from
Canada's band.

Roll on the All Blacks,
Bring on the Boks,
Move over you Wallabies,
There'll be no cup shocks!
Scotland will challenge
Against every foe.
Welsh pride in their rugby
Demands a good show.

But in the last countdown,
The form book directs,
When it comes to the final
England expects!

Bradley Waters (13)
Mounts Bay School, Penzance

Great British Stereotype

I'm a full-blooded Great British stereotype,
I can't avoid the Royal family hype,
Tea and biscuits anyone
Or buttered crumpets and chocolate buns?

I'm a full-blooded Great British stereotype,
I'll go and watch a spot of cricket
And support my local village team,
We'll be back in time for Wimbledon,
I'll watch while enjoying strawberries and cream.

I'm a full-blooded Great British stereotype,
I wear my suit and smoke my pipe,
I wear a bowler hat, shirt and tie,
I love Sunday roast and hot apple pie.

I'm a full-blooded Great British stereotype,
I say every sentence with polite manners,
I'll hold high my Union Jack banners,
I post all my letters at red postboxes
And join in the tradition of hunting for foxes.

I'm a full-blooded Great British stereotype,
But none of this is true at all,
I may live in Britain,
But way down in Cornwall.

Christopher Roberts (13)
Mounts Bay School, Penzance

What Do You Think Of?

When you think of Britain, what do you see?
You see the weather,
The horrible rain of winter
And the mildy warm sunshine of summer.

When you think of Britain, what do you smell?
You smell the fantastic fragrance of the flowers,
The extensive meadows full of real red roses
And if you sniff hard enough, maybe some
                        wonderful white roses too.

When you think of Britain, what do you taste?
You taste our sumptuous Sunday roast,
The grand gorgeous gravy
And the yummy, Yorkshire puddings,
                not forgetting British beef.

When you think of Britain, what do you hear?
You hear the hustle and bustle of the underground,
The busy network of trains taking you around London,
The echoing sounds of people talking around you.

When you think of Britain, what do you feel?
You feel like you're walking endlessly through
                        the beautiful countryside
And you feel magnificent and warm, as if you have
Somewhere to go at the end of each day,
You feel like you're . . . at home.

Daniel Bone (13)
Mounts Bay School, Penzance

England, Old And New

The English with their bowler hats,
Streets that were crowded with many rats,
Riding round on a Penny Farthing,
While little children were cold and starving,
On the streets, kids swept and slept without any pay,
Freezing day after day,
To them there's no such thing as play.

Today in England, there's none of that,
Except for the odd bloomin' rat,
Computer games are all the rage,
As well as having a pet in a cage,
Some buildings tower extremely high,
About as high as a bird can fly.

But then again something's never change,
Like in England the typical weather,
Cos rain to us is never strange.

Charlie Gardner (12)
Mounts Bay School, Penzance

Great Britain

Great Britain is full of tales
England, Scotland, Ireland, Wales
Top hats, tea bags, Sunday roast,
Lots of wine, more than most.
TV's full of soaps and soaps
All of our lost dreams and hopes,
Travelling far, more far away,
Different countries are OK,
But however far, however near,
I'd rather be anywhere but here.

Ellie Blayney (12)
Mounts Bay School, Penzance

Great Britain

G etting ready to go to the countryside,
R ed roses staring at the bright orange sun,
E very day farmers looking and waiting to harvest his crops,
A t the end of the day they go to an old English pub to have a pint,
T aking one sip at a time.

B eefeaters chewing through greasy pieces of beef,
R abbits running around with white coats,
I 'm getting married to a red rose,
T he churches are as old as a great oak tree,
A long time ago, I was just a little English boy,
I wanted to be a footballer,
N o one will beat *Great Britain*.

Gary Matthews (14)
Mounts Bay School, Penzance

Bits From Britain

Great Britain is one of the coolest places to be,
Whilst all the posh people have biscuits and tea.

Go down to Cornwall, have some clotted cream,
Then you'll start thinking you're in your own dream.

Go up to Scotland, dig into the ground,
Then come back and tell people what you had found.

The weather can be great, it can be bad,
It makes you feel happy, it makes you feel sad.

That's a bit about Britain, what do you think?
Don't write it in pencil, write it in ink.

Danielle Gorman (13)
Mounts Bay School, Penzance

A Typical Great Britain

I am a typical Great Briton,
Would you like a spot of tea?
Remember, hold your pinkie up high,
Then delicately sip.

I am a typical Great Briton,
See my pale skin and straight hair,
By the way, have a cucumber sandwich,
They're incredibly delicious.

I am a typical Great Briton,
Why do you not talk like me?
I speak with a posh accent,
I don't like yours.

I am a typical Great Briton,
That is why I travel around the world
And drink my tea,
Through my two front teeth.

Portia Thomas (13)
Mounts Bay School, Penzance

British Poem

Small Britain, little Britain, fat Britain, large,
See all those Scots in their kilts,
See all the fluffy sheep in Wales,
Small Britain, little Britain, fat Britain, large,
See all the Guinness in Northern Ireland,
See all the English breakfasts,
Small Britain, little Britain, fat Britain, large.

James Grant (14)
Mounts Bay School, Penzance

The British Isles

North is Scotland, hills and mountains high,
There is haggis which you may have tried.

South of Britain is Cornwall, beaches far and wide,
Everywhere you go, an old tin mine is nearby.

West is Ireland and Wales, where farming and fields are known,
One with sheep, one with leprechauns never shown.

Finally is east, where London lies,
In our capital, there are our royals, West Minister and Big Ben,
The Tower, the London Eye for only twenty pounds, ten.

Seaside, sightseeing, countryside where rivers flow,
English heritage, as we know.

Fish and chips, roast beef, scones and home baked bread,
Cup of tea, not forgetting English breakfast, ham and eggs.

Then there is football, rugby, hunting and cricket,
Typical English - just the ticket.

England, Ireland, Scotland and Wales,
That is our British Isles.

Lauren Hands (12)
Mounts Bay School, Penzance

Great Britain

B eautiful, bygone buildings stand in country grounds,
R ugby players pumped with power and energy,
I rish drink Guinness in the *local!*
T artan kilts and ready bagpipes,
A ncient churches with Gothic spires,
I nteriors from a Victorian era,
N ational anthem sung by all.

Hannah Jones (14)
Mounts Bay School, Penzance

England

England is known for its numerous sports,
Houses guarded like royal forts,
In the heart of England on the London Street,
The leaders of our country meet.
The fatty foods change our pace,
While we sit and watch the Ascot race,
Our posh tailor suits and bowler hats,
Our red brick houses and welcome mats.
Queen Elizabeth sits on her throne
And cats sit on their walls and moan,
The expensive cars like Bentleys and Jags,
The corner shop's packed with papers and mags,
This is our country, miserable old Britain,
So clothes to pack are scarves and mittens.

Richard Gilling (14)
Mounts Bay School, Penzance

Great Britain

G reat royals once ruled this fair land,
R omans invaded the English sand,
E ngland, Scotland, Ireland and Wales,
A ll their feuds make up historical tales,
T hroughout the ages wars carried on.

B attles fought and sometimes won,
R oyals, plagues, fires and disease,
I n ships heroes protected their seas,
T rafalgar saw Nelson die for his land,
A ll rebels in Scotland had Wallis to hand.
I rish people have peace at last,
N ation of one, forget the past.

Michael Burt (14)
Mounts Bay School, Penzance

A Place Called Great Britain

Where a gratifying queen rules the land,
With a positive royal hand . . .

Where vintage walls reach up metres high,
In tho fioldo oow and cattle lie . . .

Where Big Ben rings its bell,
So you know the time to tell . . .

Where the seagulls fly wild and free,
Flying, squawking towards the sea . . .

Where Englishmen and English women,
Have their tea at early morning . . .

At a place called Great Britain.

Elizabeth Nielsen (13)
Mounts Bay School, Penzance

Great Britain

G reat it's time for scones and tea,
R oast dinner on Sunday, *yippee*
E xcellent let's visit Buckingham Palace,
A mazing there goes the Queen,
T rains and tubes that never stop.

B angers being thrown which make them *pop*,
R hubarb and custard's the pudding of the day,
I t deserves a *hip hip hooray*,
T ime for shopping in the West End
A nd traffic speeding round the bend,
I t's good to see Big Ben standing tall,
N ow let's go to great Albert Hall.

Joe Marshall Brown (12)
Mounts Bay School, Penzance

Great Britain

Great Britain is the place to be
Full of fun, laughter, joy and glee,
It is certainly the place for me,
An island surrounded by a glittering sea.

I am lucky to live in a place like this,
Because a chance to live here would not go amiss,
Living in Britain is a dream come true,
But can only happen for a few.

Her Majesty the Queen sits on her royal throne
And rules the country all alone,
Tony Blair is our Prime Minister
And some would say he is a little sinister.

Great Britain is made up of four different nations,
England, Ireland, Scotland and Wales,
Each one sharing this vast empire,
Which is the Great Britain of our desire.

Great Britain is our island small but strong
And its history is amazing and long,
Many have heart of this kingdom so proud
Our anthem will be heard by all around.

Ross Lawrance (14)
Mounts Bay School, Penzance

Great Britain

Here we are, all crowded in the street
Nothing to do but keep on our feet,
Big Ben chimes, it's 6 o'clock and
Rush hour begins,
You think it's all calmed down,
Yet the night's as busy as the day,
It's always like this and you can't
Change the way it is,
Here in Great Britain.

Bryony Torrie (11)
Mounts Bay School, Penzance

Great Britain

Great Britain is the place to be
With its historic towns by the sea.

Fish and chips is the local dish,
As good as any heart can wish.

A win at Wimbledon is the dream
Whilst eating strawberries and cream.

On the Thames for the boat race
Coxswain shouts to keep the pace.

In Buckingham Palace lives the Queen
Greatest landmark ever seen.

Overall Great Britain is the best
Come and put us to the test.

Jack Outram (14)
Mounts Bay School, Penzance

Great Britain

England's mist clouds the sky,
Like bowler hats and big bow ties.

Ireland's lakes and fishing land,
Are owned by men known as grand.

Scottish Highlands, glisten at night
Like dust that gathers around a light.

Wales folk are known to man,
For their grumpy faces and boring land.

All these places make one big place,
Tied together like a great shoe lace.

Laura Rosewall (14)
Mounts Bay School, Penzance

Great Britain

Pinkie in the air,
While sipping the tea,
With a hint of posh accents,
Makes the Royal family.

Tea and biscuits,
Strawberries and cream,
Castles and buildings,
Filled with lots of history.

Wimbledon is here,
So come on in,
What a surprise!
We've lost once again.

Cold winter mornings,
Mild summer days,
What can you expect,
From our pale, stunned ways.

All this makes Great Britain
With our tea and crumpets,
Watch us play some cricket
For Great Britain is the best.

Jennifer Allen (13)
Mounts Bay School, Penzance

My Country

My country is posh and elegant today,
I'm sure the British would say,
But I do wonder what Great Britain was like
If I stepped back 100 years . . .

Beautiful corsets and top hats stand proud
Into the ballroom, the noble arrive,
Classical melodies, music and wine,
Adorned faces white, yet still so alive.

The scented silks and silver so common,
The joyful couples waltz through the night,
Everyone was filled with such passion and song,
But that was back then and now it's all gone.

Now my country is packed to the brim,
With empty beer cans and lager loud fans,
I really do wonder what my life would be like,
If I stepped back 100 years . . .

Hannah Bakewell (13)
Mounts Bay School, Penzance

Great Britain

England, Ireland, Scotland, Wales,
All sharing their tastes in ales,
Together we all make Britain great,
It was all really down to fate.

Everyone licks their lips,
At traditional fish and chips,
With strawberries and cream,
We are living our dream.

Living together side by side,
We made a country full of pride,
Under our traditional British weather,
We will live side by side forever.

Natalie Mitchell (14)
Mounts Bay School, Penzance

Great Britain

If you're a stranger to our country,
Then let me be your guide,
I'll take you from the north to south,
Coast to coast and countrywide.
We'll start up north in Scotland
Where haggis is the fare,
William Wallace fought for freedom,
Under kilts they're bare!
Northern mills of the revolution,
That made our nation great!
Now they're gone, forgotten
Who can tell our fate?
The great industrial centre,
The middle of our land,
Spaghetti junction, a meeting point,
For every travelling strand.
Rugby, sheep and teachers,
All chief exports from Wales,
But tourists flock to Snowdon,
To walk through hills and dales.
London is our capital,
It's trendy, hip and cool,
Big Ben, the Eye, the Palace
And home to those who rule.
And then of course there's Cornwall
The jewel in the crown,
White sands, King Arthur and cream teas,
Why don't you all come down!

Danielle Taylor (12)
Mounts Bay School, Penzance

Great Britain

G oing fishing with your dad in the early morning,
R unning round the old farm in your wellies,
E ating strawberries and cream at Wimbledon,
A t the gate of Windsor Castle waiting for the Queen,
T ime for dinner, it is roast on a Sunday evening.

B ritish love their food especially fish and chips,
R iding in the car down a country road,
I n the countryside, is where I like to be,
T winkles of sunlight on my face,
A ll the seasons in changing grace,
I nto the darkness when night-time falls,
N ight Great Britain, Big Ben has called.

Shelby Kessell (11)
Mounts Bay School, Penzance

Great Britain!

G oing to Buckingham Palace today,
R ushing to see the Queen,
E ating fish and chips,
A cting very posh,
T he Thames runs through the city.

B ig Ben tells the time,
R oudy people everywhere,
I n the London Eye,
T he Capital is London,
A ttractions all around,
I n and out the Central Park,
N earing home before it's dark.

Zoe Maiden (11)
Mounts Bay School, Penzance

England

When I think of England,
I see all sorts in my head,
Like watching a Rolls Royce,
Driving over a country cottage flower bed.

Wouldn't it be funny,
To see the Queen,
Eating fish and chips,
Or scones with jam and cream.

If you go on a journey,
To Stonehedge or the London Eye,
Watch all the American tourists,
Eating steak and kidney pie.

Oh, it would be strange,
To see Tony Blair,
Walking around
In Trafalgar Square.

Emma Collins (11)
Mounts Bay School, Penzance

Globe Theatre

G lobe Theatre, Shakespeare's word,
L ondon where his voice was heard,
O n the stage with a speech,
B y a script, he tried to reach,
E veryone sitting on edge.

T o the actors watching on the ledge,
H eroic Shakespeare for a reaction
E verybody had their satisfaction,
A ll the actors waiting in the wing
T o join in the final song, the final curtain drops and swings,
R apturous applause,
E ncore!

Jessica Leah (11)
Mounts Bay School, Penzance

Great Britain

England, Ireland,
Scotland, Wales,
Red, white, blue,
Eating fish and chips,
Drinking cups of tea,
Around the green countryside,
Beautiful sights to see,
Rain, fog and wind,
Is mostly the weather we get,
But when the sun shines,
We like to go to the beach to get wet,
Football, hockey and netball,
Some sports we play,
I'm glad I live in Great Britain
And go to school at Mount's Bay.

Yvonne Trembath (11)
Mounts Bay School, Penzance

Cornwall

C raggy cliffs to the
O range sunset,
R ocks of granite on the
N earby beaches,
W aves bring the fishermen into the harbours,
A ll the visitors come to see St Michael's Mount,
L aughing seagulls overhead,
L amps for tin miners now forgotten.

Matthew Laity (11)
Mounts Bay School, Penzance

Great Britain

Going to London is not fair
I'm never allowed to go anywhere,
Rain, sun, fog and snow,
I can't find the way to go.
Eating Cornish pasties is so great,
I could eat them till it's late,
Around to Scotland to the loch,
Seeing Nessy will give you a shock,
To the cottage of your dreams,
Have apple pie with clotted cream.

Bagpipes are played up in the north,
As the youth perform the sword dance to and forth,
Round and round the London Eye,
Get hit in the face with a big cream pie,
In and out around the town,
The May day dance is seen around,
Trains help us to get around,
From England to Wales and all around.
Around this country you will know,
That in Scotland there is snow.
In and out of buses and planes,
They help us get around just like trains,
Now to end my little rhyme,
I must go home because I have no time.

Jennifer Anne Greenslade (11)
Mounts Bay School, Penzance

Great Britain

G oing to see the changing of the guards,
R unning around with Cornish bards,
E ating fry ups every day,
A round and around on the London Eye,
T in mining next for the men.

B ong! Goes the chime of Big Ben,
R oast dinners are the best,
I n a pub in the south west,
T ea and biscuits in a cottage,
A nd fresh Wigan pie to cool,
I n the fridge,
N ow that's a country I'm proud to call home.

Jordy Glasson (11)
Mounts Bay School, Penzance

Great Britain

Go out for fish and chips,
Look at great big ships,
We have seagulls all the time,
Big Ben makes a loud chime.

Great Britain is great,
The Queen's head of state,
We have an army and a navy,
We can't eat meat without gravy.

We have Bonfire Night,
It gives people a fright,
The England football team,
Make a scream when they score a goal.

Rebecca Sedgeman (11)
Mounts Bay School, Penzance

Great Britain

G reen and grand is our land,
R ed, white and blue our flag flies for you,
E ngland, Scotland, Northern Ireland and Wales,
A re all part of Great Britain with its wonderful tales,
T ogether and united but all very different.

B ig Ben chimes in our London town,
R oyals represent us, the Queen wears a crown,
I n our separate countries we try to work as one
T ogether or none,
A ll of us have different views on how our countries
    should be run,
I n the end it all comes down to working as one
N ever along, always together our Great Britain!

Holly Stevens (11)
Mounts Bay School, Penzance

England

When I think of England
All sorts occur to me
Football, rugby, cricket
And fish and chips for tea.

Big Ben stands tall,
Houses of Parliament nearby,
The Millennium Dome didn't work,
But they might give it another try.

When I think of England,
I'd rather live here than Rome,
Because when I think of England,
I'm thinking of my home.

Chris Burt (12)
Mounts Bay School, Penzance

The Jewel In The Sea

When I think of England,
I see all sorts in my head,
I might think of London, our capital city,
Or I might think of cream teas instead,
London has all the great sights,
Buckingham Palace or Big Ben at night.

I am British, I don't know why
My sense of pride makes me fly so high,
This little isle, a jewel in the sea,
Crammed full of chips, roast beef and tea.

Hooray for dear old England
We stand so tall and proud,
Let's go to Speaker's Corner
And shout it all around.

Alex Jones (11)
Mounts Bay School, Penzance

Baby Boy

What is that I hear?
I'm sure it's a cry of fear,
I go towards the cry,
Of a little boy,
Who would have left him here?
Well they obviously didn't care,
Who would do such a thing
To an innocent baby boy?
It looked like he was abandoned
And wasn't meant to be found
And I wonder if before they left,
They gave him a little kiss,
But just think left here to die
And what if I didn't hear his cry?
It just makes me wonder
Was he left to die?

Vikki Rostock (13)
Poltair Community School & Sports College, St Austell

Waterfalls

When I was on holiday
I kicked my ball
I chased after it, and
It fell into the waterfall.

So I decided there and then,
To jump in like a great buffoon,
I felt like a real fool,
But it popped up real soon.

All my friends thought it was cool,
As I was falling, I noticed something really odd,
When I realised and thought about it,
It was shiny, silver, red and blue,
'Oh my God' - it was gems.

I thought to myself through the rest of the day,
Shall I go back and get the gems or
Shall I go to the beach and play?
We returned to the beach,
But there was nothing, there was nothing there,
Now each time I see a waterfall,
I stop and stare, and each time I make a friend
It reminds me of the past, and how I jumped from the waterfall,
As I hit the water very fast, it reminded me about the times
I've had messing about in the water and being happy and glad.

Emma Griffin (13)
Poltair Community School & Sports College, St Austell

The World Of Motion

Standing in the sun,
Watching the world go by,
The world is motion,
I hear you cry,
An action can change,
How you feel
Turning on,
The motion wheel,
Who can stop this?
Full of hate,
Love and emotion,
One day this
World will flow,
To keep the motion
Going slow.

David Neville (12)
Poltair Community School & Sports College, St Austell

Robin Reliant Poem

As it struggles down the road,
It makes some sort of engine code,
It rocks around and makes a sound.

It only has three wheels
And jumps around like seals,
It bounces up and down and makes the public frown.

It flies down the hill,
Like it's on the kill,
But up a hill it cannot cope
And has no hope, it's a *Robin Reliant!*

Ben Douglas (12)
Poltair Community School & Sports College, St Austell

Crash And Burn

Wheels turning
Engines roaring
Two young lads
Hearts soaring.

Racing each other
On a dirt track
Laugh together
And then turn back.

Wheels stop turning
Engines groaning
Two young lads
Both stopped moving.

Lost control
And overturned
Over and over
Crashed and burned.

Forward motion
Faster and faster
For the inexperienced
Only disaster.

Slow down
Don't go too fast,
Make your life count
Make it last.

Scott Wiley (12)
Poltair Community School & Sports College, St Austell

Travelling

The crash of the waves against the rugged rocks,
A boat at anchor bobbing up and down in the troughs,
The wind blows the trees and leaves fall to the ground
And they're scattered around,
The wind gets fast and blows people around,
It spins and swerves never knowing where to go.
A horse in a field travelling end to end,
The floor rumbling because of his hooves,
Its mane is blowing back from its face,
As it breaks into a canter and picks up his pace.
A cheetah running to catch his prey,
Sprinting as fast as it can,
A zebra runs and dodges side to side
And in the end the zebra is relieved it ran.
As a tornado travels, it goes around and around,
It travels on land and on water,
Wrecking houses and trees as it goes on its way,
So the children no longer play.
The running river going so fast with fish jumping into the air,
Then it falls off the edge of the rock and turns into a waterfall
And plunges into a wide shallow pool.
A sleepy head pops out of a shell,
It eats some grass then doodles along,
He looks around for something else to eat,
There's nothing there, so he goes back to sleep.

Leah Emerson (12)
Poltair Community School & Sports College, St Austell

Windy Days

The tall stems of bamboo
Sway fiercely to and fro
As if they'd like to leave
But don't know where to go.

The weather cock on high
Jerks just as fiercely too
It whirls up in the sky
Not knowing what to do.

Electric wires on their poles
Swing sharp from side to side
They dash about as fast
As on a theme park ride.

The flames in the bonfire
Flicker and flutter fast
Smoke billows up in clouds
See how it rushes past.

The washing on the line
Flaps and flies around
The canvas on our tent
Makes a loud clapping sound.

Chantel Bishop (12)
Poltair Community School & Sports College, St Austell

The Football Match

At the football match,
Everyone running,
After the black and white ball,
People cheering all the time.
Atmosphere. Loads of shouting and
Cheering and booing.
Scoring goals jumping around cheering,
All the supporters are feeling so good
Excited and the other fans upset and booing.

Aaron Crocker (13)
Poltair Community School & Sports College, St Austell

Running Motion Poem

As I step up to the track just about to start the race,
I was very determined, you could see it on my face.
Everyone started running, I needed to pick the pace,
My legs felt as if I was gonna fall flat on my face.

I was too slow, I still had a long way to go,
But I said to myself, *I'm gonna win I know!*
Someone has to lose oh well
So ouch! I fell and hurt my toe
And I almost took after someone, oh no!

I start to run faster, faster and faster,
But my toe really hurts, I think I need a plaster!
I can do this, I am the running master
Even though the start of the race was a disaster.

Yes! I've nearly finished the race, I knew it wouldn't be so bad
This is the hardest race I've ever had
To have run this far I must be mad
When this is over I'm gonna be so glad!

Natalie Henderson (13)
Poltair Community School & Sports College, St Austell

Movement On The Earth

Shooting star like a roller coaster
    zooming round the track.
Cloud, sun and moon move round
    the Earth as it spins.
A cheetah trying to catch its prey
    like a flash of lightning.
Heartbeat pumping fast as you're
    running round the track.
Car going 100 miles per hour down the road,
    like a rocket taking off.

Rachel Olsen (12)
Poltair Community School & Sports College, St Austell

Motion Poem

Back and forward, up and down
Eating up the open ground,
Passing others on the course
Forget I'm on a rocking horse.

Now I'm in a rowing boat
How I hope my craft will float,
Must avoid those hidden rocks
Can't smash up this cardboard box.

Lapping everyone in sight,
On my brand new motorbike,
Taking the chequered flag and then
Fall off Mother's chair again.

Mountaineering what a climb
Must get to the top in time,
Breathing gear and distress flares
Should now make it up the stairs.

Matthew May (12)
Poltair Community School & Sports College, St Austell

Motion

Slowly the wheels start turning,
creaking, squeaking, picking up speed.
Faster and faster until it went
zooming, zooming past the houses,
the hills, the flowers, the weeds.
Brakes applied, slowing, slowing,
squeaking, creaking, hills and houses
no longer zooming.
Slowing, slowing.

Ben Rowse (12)
Poltair Community School & Sports College, St Austell

Rain

Rain dripping, rain dropping,
beating on the ground,
rolling down the drainpipes
and ending on the ground.

Dripping on my umbrella,
splashing on my shoes,
dripping off my nose
and ending on the hose.

Splish splashing, splish splashing
making great big puddles
watching all the rain
as they end in great big huddles.

Birds go to find shelter,
my cat jumps in a bush
I had better go now
because it's wet and cold as well.

Melissa Lobb (12)
Poltair Community School & Sports College, St Austell

Cars

Cars that are fast
with body kits galore
and big beefy exhausts
neon lights light up the night
nitrode cars with ice galore
three spoke, four spoke, five spoke more
silver, black, gold and more
that is alloy galore.

Peter Megarry (13)
Poltair Community School & Sports College, St Austell

The Cheetah

Cheetahs running as fast as they can,
Their legs moving around and around
They're leaping up and down,
Through the grass as they can,
There it is its prey,
Bouncing around in the hay.
Can the cheetah get it
Or can the cheetah fight it?
Well it's time to find out
The cheetah's standing there on its own,
Maybe it might groan,
But the cheetah has to get it,
So the cheetah moves forward and forward.
Then . . .
The cheetah bounces on the prey
Not catching any of the hay
Then in one big bite the prey is gone,
No more squeals from the prey as it is gone,
Gone forever.

Hannah Pink (13)
Poltair Community School & Sports College, St Austell

Motion

The wind, it blew, the birds flew by
They wanted to land,
But were blown up high.

In the city the people rushed
Past each other, onto the bus
The taxis hooted, the cars, they tooted
And everyone was in a rush.

Her child was ill with chickenpox
Scabs in her hair, that fell in locks.
Mum's hands were steady in the motion
As she gently applied the calamine lotion.

Bethany Chard (13)
Poltair Community School & Sports College, St Austell

Traffic Jam

I was sat in my bedroom window watching the traffic fly by.
Then all of a sudden the traffic started to *slow down.*
It got slower and slower until it came to a halt.
I got out of my window ledge
And stepped onto my bedroom floor,
I swiftly walked to my bedroom door
And stopped to ask myself
Why have they all stopped?
I opened my bedroom door and carried on walking.
I got to the bottom of the stairs
And shouted to Mum, 'Just popping up the road.'
I slammed the front door, and ran up the road.
Some of the people in the cars
Were beeping their horns,
Others on their mobiles.
I got to the top of the road
And found out the traffic
Was being held up by a *huge* digger
Slowly going up the road.
I stopped the digger and told him
That he was causing a traffic jam.
He pulled over the traffic started moving again,
By the time I had got back to my bedroom window
The traffic was flying by smiling
Thanks to me.

Jess Ball (12)
Poltair Community School & Sports College, St Austell

Puppet Strings

She chose to walk alone though many wondered why.
She kept her eyes fixed to a dark dusty sky.
She walked past villages ruled by queens and kings.
She walked like she was pulled by imaginary puppet strings.
She wished to be a bird so that she could fly free . . .
She wished to be a boat and sail through a quay she
Straggled on her way wishing to be free,
But a dark dusty sky was all that she could see.
As she walked eyes to the sky,
Hopes at being free still held high.
As she walked the dusty street the wind swept by,
Holding on to her hops she let out a silent sigh.
Could someone help her set her free?
Answer her silent sigh, 'Someone help me.'
The whole world passed by but nothing she could do,
As a clouded lane is what she walked through.
She never blinked eyes fixed to the sky
And with one sound of laughter a tear fell from her eye.
She walked along the coast and down into the town . . .
She tore her eyes from the sky and finally looked down,
Down onto the gravel which lay upon the street,
As the sweat fell from her head in the blazing heat.
'Set me free,' she sighed looking to the ground,
But no one helped her, no one made a sound.
She walked as if being pulled by her puppet strings,
Why can't she go to Heaven upon angels' wings?
She looked back up to the dusty sky
And with a song in her heart began to cry
No one ever helped her, eyes still to the sky
She will be pulled by her puppet strings till the day she will die.

Sara McFeat (14)
Poltair Community School & Sports College, St Austell

Time

Time goes on forever riding,
Won't cease, won't stop, just abiding.

Days turn to weeks, to months, to years
Then rot away to silent tears.

Time crushes mountains, wears down stone,
Grinds granite to the bone.

Floods cities, buries towns,
Turns trees to sawdust mounds.

Will drown more lands with mighty surf
Will destroy our loving Earth.

Will end life at its picking,
But time will go on, *ticking, ticking.*

Joe Parkinson (13)
Poltair Community School & Sports College, St Austell

My Candy Ran

I bought a new kitten
I loved her so much,
She is so small I fear to touch,
Her golden coat shines in the sun,
I named her Candy after her mum,
As she got older
She could now walk and run,
She ran into the garden
In the blazing sun,
She ran into the street
And got hit by a lorry,
She slowly got up and
She just ran and ran,
I never saw her after she ran.

Laura Jago (13)
Poltair Community School & Sports College, St Austell

The Glider

It sailed off the big oak tree in a gust of wind,
Flew high in the air and whirled around in the breeze,
Glided along, over the gently rolling hills,
Saw the fields full of golden wheat, their heads looking at the sun,
Trees swaying to and fro to the rhythm of the wind,
Soared up in the air, then plunged down on its prey,
Landed on the branch of a tree in the wood,
Didn't move again until the wind picked up,
Billowed and curled as the wind moved around,
Flew off in the breeze, moved out of the wood,
Started floating down as the breeze stopped,
Reached the ground, it stood still for a while,
The draught gently blew and it scuttled around,
Scuttled along to the river bank, with a *splash* jumped in,
Heard the water scatter and trickle,
Saw the clear water sparkle and ripple,
Felt the river twist and bend,
Floated along, over waterfalls too,
Soon carried by a bluster of wind,
Fluttering about, soaked to the bone,
It landed and the sun took pity,
So shone warmly to dry it off,
It is not a blue tit, nor falcon, nor kestrel,
This poem tells the story of a simple brown leaf.

Laura Mathews (13)
Poltair Community School & Sports College, St Austell

28 Days To An Eternity

28 days is the circle of the moon
Blue moon, lunar eclipse, ruler of the tides is 'la lune'
Waxing and waning, crescent, half and full
All water's motion is ruled by this pull

Neap tides, spring tides, high tides and low
The ebb and the flow
The tidal grace
The moon's white gaze in all night's place
Magnetic pull, nature's own laws of motion
Except their strength on Earth's great ocean

The water table rises with the moon's epic power
Influencing tree, plant, animal and flower
The moon is consigned to an eternity of motion
Never really resting from her life's devotion.

Jess Mitchell (13)
Poltair Community School & Sports College, St Austell

Movement

The whistling of the trees.
The leaves swishing and swaying in the fast wind.
The birds were gliding up and down in the wind,
Soaring high in the sky.

The bike was flying by
Like a rocket in the sky.

The Ferris wheel at the fair
Goes round and round like a Catherine wheel.

Aeroplanes looping the loop
Like a white knuckle ride on a roller coaster.

Jonathan Keast (13)
Poltair Community School & Sports College, St Austell

The Way She Moves

Today's the day our two hearts will meet,
We won't know till we pass in the street,

Our hearts will tingle,
We'll no longer be single,

Our eyes will meet,
We'll feel it in our feet,

We'll be together at last,
We'll have forgotten the past,

We'll be flying high,
We'll be touching the sky,

But when the time comes,
We'll never say 'goodbye'.

We'll never shed a tear,
As long as we never fear,

If we do,
It will all be through,

I will walk alone,
I'll no longer have a home,

You'll have took it all,
Until you get an awaiting call,

It will be the call you always dread,
It'll be the one that says . . .
. . . 'Your husband's dead!'

Matthew Bale (13)
Poltair Community School & Sports College, St Austell

A Day Upon The Beach

I sat upon a sandy beach,
Just looking out to sea,
I saw a ship go sailing by,
It looked quite big to me.

It soon reached the horizon,
It disappeared out of sight,
That ship will still be travelling,
All throughout the night.

The sun shone bright upon the sea,
The water glitter brightly,
I sat just watching the waves,
Break upon the beach so lightly.

The sun had quickly faded,
The sea was not so bright,
All that there was to see,
Were shadows fading out.

It turned quite cool
And rather windy,
There's nothing else to see,
So I packed up all my things
And headed home for tea.

Shaun Collings (13)
Poltair Community School & Sports College, St Austell

Motion

Motion she goes on without noticing it,
It's always there,
Taken for granted, forgotten,
But still there,
Years pass,
She's enjoyed love, been happy, sad,
Just realising,
Her motion becomes motionless.

Rebecca Pascoe (13)
Poltair Community School & Sports College, St Austell

Weather

As the trees swayed side to side
Some leaves fell off and drifted through the sky
Some leaves are red, orange, green and brown
As they slowly float to the ground
A gust of wind came flying by,
Picked many up took them high
A cat came by with delight
Saw the leaves swirling by, he jumped up high
Caught a leaf from the blue sky
As the dark clouds come one sunny day.
As it slowly started to rain
It rained so hard thunder was formed
It struck the sky, passed the window frame
Was I to blame for this day?
I wish the sun would shine over the bay.

Lucy Cornelius (13)
Poltair Community School & Sports College, St Austell

All By The Sea

As I walk by the sea
All the things that I see
People walking, people running
All by the sea.

On the sea the boats are swaying
And rocking on the waves
Cars are skidding
Trees are rustling
All by the sea.

Birds are gliding
Clocks are ticking
People talking
All by the sea.

Claire Sowden (14)
Poltair Community School & Sports College, St Austell

'Flying' High

Here it comes the last play of the game
With a pass from the point guard
He takes it with authority
And starts to drive it hard

Dummies the first with the greatest of ease
He's really going fast
Spins round the second like he's not even there
No need to pause or pass

7, 6, 5 seconds 4
He's soaring through the air
He has to sink it there's no other way
This for the game his only real care

All eyes on him no concentration
On anything else at all
Not even on the ticking clock
Up there on the wall

The buzzer goes
The lights seem dim
But the ball hasn't dropped
It's still on the rim

The crowd's on their feet
They're gasping in awe
The ball drops down through
Followed by a great roar

He has really done it
He's won them the game
And from now on also
They shall know his name.

Tom Richardson (14)
Poltair Community School & Sports College, St Austell

The Last Goodbye

His hands shaking as he wrote his note,
His pulse jumping over hurdles,
Sealed, put on the shelf to be found.
His eyes watering, his chest tightening,
Feeling dizzy, up he stepped.
His sweat dripped, dropped, dripped,
His hands rose and his brain froze,
Was this the end?
He made up his mind, his heart pounded,
His foot slipped, *argh* he'd gone!
Down down down flying like a bird,
Bang, blood, red blood on the grey brick wall.
Swish swash swish,
The breeze from the fall moved the trees.
He was heading for the ground.
He hit the ground, dead as a doornail,
As still as the night.
Waiting for someone, someone to find him.

Alison Sturtridge (13)
Poltair Community School & Sports College, St Austell

Not A Word

They walked along the lanes together
The sky was dotted with stars
They reached the iron rails together
He lifted up the bars,
She neither smiled nor thanked him
In any way nor how,
For he was the farmer's boy
And she, the Jersey cow.

Ben Robinson (13)
Poltair Community School & Sports College, St Austell

He's Running Away Again

There he goes running again.
He's running to relieve his pain.
He's been running away from me for years.
He's trying to lose all his fears.

He starts now to walk.
He's beginning to want to talk.
He's walking now slower.
His pain is getting lower.

He's now stopped walking
He's finally started talking.
He expects me to walk to him now.
He wants to be my father again,
But he doesn't know how.

My father's now alright with me.
I keep walking over there for tea.
We are now running together.
He's started running ahead again.

Andrew Phillimore (13)
Poltair Community School & Sports College, St Austell

Autumn

The summer is now over,
The leaves are turning brown,
I stare at all the trees,
I wonder and I frown.
Why the leaves are falling,
Fluttering in the sky,
They're yellow, brown and orange,
Why, oh why, oh why?
Because now it's autumn,
The nights are getting dark,
So the leaves keep falling,
In the town and in the park.

Aleisha Page (14)
Poltair Community School & Sports College, St Austell

Weird Birds

As it soared through the sky
Its colours brightly caught my eye.
It landed with a big *thump*
It made all the other criminals jump.
They scattered like flies,
The bird lay sideways and cried.
Its wings seemed to be damaged,
When I came it flew and fell like a cabbage.
Its beak was sharp
From fishing for carp.
It said its name was Mark
And loved jogging at the pair.
It fixed its wings,
It then started to sing.
It flew in the sky
And chirped goodbye.

Louis Wakley (13)
Poltair Community School & Sports College, St Austell

Disco

The pumping of the music,
The thumping of my head,
They're moving to the beat,
The stamping of their feet.

The twizzles and the twirls,
The spins and the swirls,
The laughing and the giggles,
The spinning and the wiggles.

The jazz and the pop,
I don't want it to stop,
The dancing round the clock,
I won't stop till I drop.

Rebecca Ringrose (13)
Poltair Community School & Sports College, St Austell

Bridge View!

I looked down at the water,
Swish, swosh, swish,
I just stood there watching my life drift away.
I thought about the way Dad had hit me,
My head throbbing, my nose bleeding,
The way Mum had screamed and shouted,
How many bruises would she have tomorrow.
Argh! The pain is too much!
My cheeks are wet with tears,
What would life be like for little Emma and Ross?
'What the . . . ?'
A hand was resting on my shoulder,
I turned around and saw him,
The monster, eyes as red as fire
What do I do now?
I can't leave Mum with him,
'Hey!'
Argh!
Splash.

Tamsin Moor (13)
Poltair Community School & Sports College, St Austell

Clouds Forever!

Clouds! Clouds are fluffy white
Glistening in the sun,
Passing over land and sea,
Just building up into a cumulus
Until they become as one.
Clouds stacking mile upon mile high,
Shapes form pictures as I stare into the sky!

Dave Colliver (13)
Poltair Community School & Sports College, St Austell

Take Me!

Come with me, take my hand
To a place we understand
Walk with me, I'll show you how
To live in peace here and now.

Come with me, come in my world
Relax, be calm, no bombs are hurled
People hush, please calm down
Please don't wave, stop the frown.

Move with me, stop the tears
Run with me, we'll drown your fears
In my world, no people die
There's no reason for you to cry.

Follow me, I'll stay with you
Sit down here, we'll talk it through
Come with me, walk this way
Sit down here, don't run away.

Anna Borlase (14)
Poltair Community School & Sports College, St Austell

The Sand Grain's Dream

I am a little sand grain, that no one cares about,
I get trod into humans' shoes and sometimes can't get out.

I am so small and tiny I get washed out by tide
And sometimes I get really scared and find a place to hide.

I am so very frightened and also very shy
And other sand grains bully me, I feel like I could die.

I just wish I was bigger, as big as big can be
And I would be so brave and strong that no one could beat me.

I'd stay in when the tide went out,
So everyone could see, that the bravest little sand grain
Is definitely *me!*

Caroline Wilhelmsen (13)
Poltair Community School & Sports College, St Austell

I Am Moving

I am moving through the city,
Translucent smog in the air,
Tears falling down her face,
So soft, so young, so fair.

I am moving through the woodland,
Greenery all around,
Wondering what I've done,
Wondering where I'm bound.

I am moving through the beach,
People full of laughter,
I used to go there with her,
But not since after . . .

I am moving up the motorway,
A place I'm often on,
Off to another care home,
Mummy, where have you gone?

Sam Roseveare (13)
Poltair Community School & Sports College, St Austell

Island Tourists

It is the summer season,
The population has almost doubled,
The walking road blocks march across the streets,
They are like warts on your face,
As we ride down the hills,
Shouting as loud as we can,
Out come the twitchers,
Taking lots of pictures,
The black of the night brought trouble to the street,
People scared of their own shadows,
The moon glows looking over the islands,
Like a lighthouse as a warning,
Scanning across the horizon,
Ending at the double hills of Samson.

Alex Nel (14)
Poltair Community School & Sports College, St Austell

My Usual Day

The noisy door opens slowly,
At this time I know it's going to be a usual day,
One step at a time,
It takes me to sit in my usual seat.

The bus is so slow,
I look out the window, watching what
I normally watch every day.

Everybody chatting to their friends,
As I sit on my own thinking about life.

The bus pulls up
And as we miserably walk off,
We say bye to the bus driver.

It's going to be a usual day.

Eve Leaney (12)
Poltair Community School & Sports College, St Austell

Car Superstar!

Sitting in silence,
I'm here safe and still,
Sat between the cushions,
Now it's time to chill.

The engine roars,
As the trees walk on by,
Flashing lights, wander the sky.
As we speed up, my heart is in my throat,
Then he looks at me, and I float.
There to rescue me, in that car,
He sits and waits
My superstar!

Willow Groechel (13)
Poltair Community School & Sports College, St Austell

My Grampy

My grampy fussed over me,
When I was young.
When I got dirty,
He always brushed me down.

I don't remember much,
As he went into a home.
I visited him a lot.
He sat by the window and looked out over the sea.

He had a friend called Polly,
So he was never alone.
I loved my grampy so much,
I wish he was still alive.

We remember him with white *lilies,*
I miss him
        so
            much.

Clare Stubbs (12)
Poltair Community School & Sports College, St Austell

Passing Time

Rain pattering on the grass,
Little raindrops shimmering like glass,
Then comes the silence as the moon rises fast,
To light up the puddles created on the path,
Hours later dawn rises,
Casting early shadows,
The new day full of surprises.

Fran Price (13)
Poltair Community School & Sports College, St Austell

The Maths Block Mosh

It's three o'clock
We're on the edge of our seats
We await the bell that sets us free

Eyes locked on the clock
We all sit and wait
Until it reaches five past three

The bell it sounds
We jump from our seats
And down the stairs we go!

Like a pack of hounds
We mash and pound
And in amazement we all shout *whoa!*

Bundle!
The riot begins
And we sprint to join in the action

Just like a gumball
We smash and tumble
As we all join in the faction!

Grant Coles (12)
Poltair Community School & Sports College, St Austell

Fireworks

Fireworks spread across the night sky
Like a darting firefly.
As the rocket fired the night got tired,
Balls of fire spitting through the air
Sparks alight be aware.

Jack Best (12)
Poltair Community School & Sports College, St Austell

The Nightmare

I jog, I run, I sprint,
But it doesn't seem to take the hint.
The dullness looks like it will never end,
Slowly slipping into bend after bend.

I feel myself tipping,
Dripping, skipping,
Goes the sweat on my face,
I cannot move as if I'm a solid glass case.

The ground begins to tilt,
Just like a rose I'm afraid I will wilt.
I start to roll, roll and roll,
Up ahead I see nothing but its soul.

Faster and faster my heart does beat,
As I look around I begin to feel the heat.
Rushing through the air,
Streaming through my hair.

As I jog, run then sprint,
It feels as though it's taking the hint.
I gaze into the gloom,
I open my eyes to see my bedroom.

Charlotte Spry (14)
Poltair Community School & Sports College, St Austell

World Cup Glory

Foul, penalty the ball is on the spot
Staying absolutely still
Beckham steps up
To score against Brazil

It's the 89th minute
The tension is rising
The crowd are chanting
Whilst Brazil are moaning and grunting

The whistle touches the ref's lips
The penalty's about to be taken
The whole team is nervous
Waiting for it to be taken

Beckham approaches the ball
And strikes it mighty clean
It twirls and curls
Then hits the net, England are one up
With one minute left

England look to the ref
To see if the game is finished
All of a sudden the whistle is blown
Brazil's hopes are diminished

At last they have done it,
England have won it
We've finally achieved World Cup glory
That's the end of this amazing story.

Ryan McMillan (13)
Poltair Community School & Sports College, St Austell

I Am A Wave Of Horses

Like a hammer on an anvil,
I crash against the rocks.
I hit, retreat, then hit again,
Sometimes I shake the docks.

Usually I am a calm herd . . .
But I can be a raging stampede.
I can destroy anything in my path,
From rock to delicate seaweed.

I'm extremely dangerous,
I'm constant like the sun.
I am as strong as 1,000 oxen,
My job is never done!

I'm always eroding and wearing things down
I turn great rocks into sand
I am never satisfied . . .
Like a file, I reshape the land.

Annelise Harris (12)
Poltair Community School & Sports College, St Austell

The Spirit Of My Friend

The freshness of his breath, lingers through the air,
the way his fingertips run in my hair,
the way his hands move when he talks to me,
the way which he walks down a crowded street.

The soft, slow way he touches my skin,
the mysterious ways he thinks within,
the way he laughs with his head tilted back,
the way his movements are so relaxed.

The way he runs, the way he walks,
the way he laughs, the way he talks,
the way that he's special, the way he's a friend,
the way that he'll be there to the very end.

Natalie Dingle (13)
Poltair Community School & Sports College, St Austell

The Sea!

The sea is like a fierce lion,
Running as fast as the wind.
Sometimes it is gentle as a bird,
Flying softly like gentle breezes.
It moves quickly as a leopard,
Storming past the trees.
When the lightning comes it is
A sports car screaming by!
Waves are 10 feet tall,
Like a giraffe walking slowly past.
A boat sail smoothly across,
Quickly, quietly like a
Predator looking for its prey!
In the sea,
Fishes are swimming furiously,
To the ocean's floor bed.
The sea is for people,
Swimming swiftly away from danger.
But the sea,
Will always be a fierce lion,
Running as fast as the wind!

Alex Baker (12)
Poltair Community School & Sports College, St Austell

Football Crazy

The ball is kicked the crowd cheers
All the men clash their beers

The ball is struck what a goal!
Oh no, the ball's been stolen!

The ball is played for a counter attack!
Ouch! What a smack.

The game is postponed because of the weather.
Oh well never mind, it's better late than never.

Michael Moreland (12)
Poltair Community School & Sports College, St Austell

Going Through The Motions

The tide rising and falling,
Like a little baby breathing.
As the sun and moon
Float across the sky,
Dawn turns to dusk
And dusk to dawn.
The motion,
Of time.

The subtle, skulky sea creatures,
Scuttle here and there,
To find cover from the thunderous feet above.
Slimy seaweed slithers by,
Curling, clawing, clinging.
Trying desperately to grasp you
And tear you out of your world,
Into darkness.

Waves crashing, smashing, splashing,
As the white horses' mouths froth,
Like bubbles in a bathtub.
The salty sea spray stinging you in the face,
Like the agonising sobs of grief,
Over a lost loved one.
The sea, the sky, the world,
Is just an endless motion.

Alison Sirley (12)
Poltair Community School & Sports College, St Austell

30 Minutes To Go

The sun rises,
The bus drivers awaken,
I step out of my house
And I start walking down the road to the bus stop.

I hope the bus,
I hope the bus won't come,
I look at the time, five past eight,
25 minutes left,
Each day I hope the bus doesn't come,
But it does.

10 past,
The time the devil bus will come,
But it doesn't, I am happy,
Will it come?

20 past,
I get ready to run home,
No sign of the bus,
But then a bus comes down the hill but drives right past.
It wasn't my bus.

29 past,
I am at my door about to open it,
10 seconds left
10, 9, 8, 7, 6, 5, 4, 3, 2 . . .
And the bus comes down the hill
And stops in front of me.
The driver opens the doors and cries out, 'Welcome.'

Martin Chapman (12)
Poltair Community School & Sports College, St Austell

Sea

The waves crash
Against the cliff
The white froth running
Like white horses galloping

The trees rustling
Against each other
Leaves are fluttering
Like butterflies in summer

The children laughing
Like in the playground
It's a shame that they
Are on the seabed.

Leanne Casson (12)
Poltair Community School & Sports College, St Austell

Tiger, Tiger

Tiger creep up on your prey,
In the dark or light of day.
Run, run, faster, faster,
He's gaining, gaining, now he'll kill you.

If he gets you he will pounce,
No time to scream, shout, announce.
He'll just kill you,
Again and again, through and through.

If you start running now,
He's got no chance, no matter how,
Fast, fast, fast he runs,
Unless the poacher's got a gun.

Jasmyn Ralph (13)
Poltair Community School & Sports College, St Austell

The Bouncy Ball

I'm a small, round and colourful bouncy ball,
Bouncing all around,
I bounce here, I spring there,
Right up into the clear, clean air,
I spin, bound, jump and swizz,
I'm bounced so high I nearly disappear,
Help, I'm frightened,
Boing, boing, boing
I'm lost, I'm in a ditch
The leaves crunch and scrunch,
It's cold, it's wet,
I'm now sat still,
Please don't leave me here,
I want to be thrown and bounced high again
And played with, not stay still.

Bradley Tresidder (11)
Poltair Community School & Sports College, St Austell

Silently But Slowly

Silently, but slowly the grey clouds sail by.
Cradled by the blue silk sky
Under the rain exclaimed its arrival
Upon the sullen faces as they frown
Child after child scurry by.
Whilst adult after adult herd them to and fro,
But as the rain comes to a standstill
The sullen faces smile
Watching the silent but slow clouds sail by.

Charlotte Owens (12)
Poltair Community School & Sports College, St Austell

Motion Of My Lips

Only the motion of my lips
Can describe the movement of these things:
On the sea
Boats are swaying,
Jumping the waves
Or rocking gently from side to side,
People walking, talking,
Barefoot on the sand,
Children laughing,
Flying kites,
Building sandcastles all day long,
Beach balls are flying,
Here, there and everywhere,
People screaming!
Shouting!
Talking,
Whispering,
Shhhh
Only the motion of my lips
Can describe the movement of these things.

Leaha Hale (13)
Poltair Community School & Sports College, St Austell

Moto GP

The bike flies around the corner at the speed of light
They go so quick
The speed dial clicks
The heatmeter glows
The bike flows
As it wheelies off the ground
It makes a thunderous sound
As it races down the straight
Make sure you don't brake too late
As he falls to the ground
The crowd makes a roaring sound.

Tom Martin (13)
Poltair Community School & Sports College, St Austell

Motion

All this too-ing and fro-ing
And coming and going
Pushing and pulling
And running and slowing
I kinda have this notion
That all this stuff is motion.
You open your eye
Look up to the skies
Breathe in and out
And without a doubt
That's when I had this notion
This stuff was also motion
When you chew your grub
Or wash in the tub
When you cook or clean
Even if you have a dream
When you write with a pen
This is motion again.
No matter where you are
If you eat, or if you learn
If you run, hop, skip or walk
If you're quiet or you talk
If you just sit and watch the ocean
You must can't escape motion.
Motion is everywhere you go
Sometimes it's fast, sometimes it's slow
But for the world to survive.
For every person to be alive
One thing we all should know
Motion, we need motion or we'd all be dead you know.

Ashley Burr (14)
Poltair Community School & Sports College, St Austell

The Stormy Sea

Looking from the harbour
I watched the choppy waves
Splashing up against the wall
Making people back away

The water lapped against the rocks
While the wind carried spray
The sea mist made my face quite wet
What a windy day!

Every once so often
A cold wave would come
And splash me through the railings
Making me all numb!

I saw a yacht bobbing up and down
Struggling with the gale
The motion proved to be too much
For the windswept sail.

Emma Sleeman (11)
Poltair Community School & Sports College, St Austell

Death A Step Away

As the rain bolts down from the shadowed clouds,
Blackness drifts across the land,
A fiery ball scoots through the sky
And falls upon the ground.
As the fire runs through the forest trees
They burn like a sting from a bumblebee.
The cheetah sprints to catch his prey,
The owl swoops to kill,
The deer run, pounce and play,
Death is one step away!

Nicola Cornelius (12)
Poltair Community School & Sports College, St Austell

A Dolphin

As the dolphin leapt up over the waves,
He jumped gracefully and peacefully,
Up and up he went,
Soaring like an eagle,
Flying through the air.

He went down with a big *splash!*
Down to the surface,
Cutting through the waves like a hot knife cutting through butter,
Down to see his fishy friends,
Underneath the water.

He swam out far from the island,
He was swimming so fast and quick and impatient,
He was swimming towards the rock,
The bump on his head appeared.

The water started to ripple,
Up the dolphin came,
The water dripping off him,
As he talked in gladness,
The water surrounded him.

All I could see was his body in mid-air,
His smiling face looking at me,
So cute I wish he was mine,
Diving in and out of the water he talked,
It was as if he knew me.

He felt a bit lonely out there all on his own,
A bit scared that he has an enemy waiting to get him,
Just waiting . . . waiting to get him,
Somewhere he felt something missing,
Something in his heart was missing.

Zoe Dunstan (11)
Poltair Community School & Sports College, St Austell

Motion

Walking by the winding river,
The autumnal weather
Makes me shiver,
I'm walking briskly,
Over the red and gold leaves.

Crunching and crispy,
The winding river weaves,
I stroll along the river bank,
The tree branches are nearly bare,
I start to run and skip,
Throwing pebbles along the way.

I suddenly stop
And look all around me,
The clouds are heavy and black,
The rain drizzles softly.

Nina Collins (11)
Poltair Community School & Sports College, St Austell

Motion Poem

This morning I woke up feeling quite low,
Down the stairs I went very slow.
I hurried to the gym
And put on my kit,
Then started my training to get very fit.
Off to play football with my mate,
He wouldn't like if I was late.
One kick of the ball it went so high,
It went over the crossbar into the sky.

Ryan Henderson (12)
Poltair Community School & Sports College, St Austell

The Cheetah

What speed, as the cheetah whistles through the air
Faster than a flare
That 60 miles per hour
What power!

He's not gonna stop
Go get him cop
See him fly
You won't stop him, so don't try.

No way he will rest
Because he is the best
Watch him burn that track
You won't ever get a glimpse of his back.

He's too fast to leave a trail
And too fast to catch his tail
Don't you dare get in his path
If you think you can stop him you're havin' a laugh.

The zooming cheetah is his name
I wouldn't try and play his game
He lands his prey and all goes black
You can see him saying *I'll be back!*

Terry Boswell (11)
Poltair Community School & Sports College, St Austell

Hunting

Swiftly through the long dry grass
Bush leaves rustle she goes so fast

Wind blows through her speckly fur
She sees her prey *grrr*

There's the herd, it's time to stop
She hides behind a great big rock

She makes a noise, the chase is on.

Anna Southey (12)
Poltair Community School & Sports College, St Austell

The Journey

I slowly moved down the road,
My engine sounded bad,
My driver kept me going,
I thought it would never end.

I drove down the road,
I went *bump, bump, bump,*
I skidded around,
Around and around.

The rain beat down on me,
My engine was playing up,
I sluggishly chugged down the road,
I didn't think I would get through this.

I felt like a drowned rat,
As my shiny skin was being dampened,
I thought that things
Couldn't be worse.

I bumped up and down,
Like a jumping machine,
I was splashed at by the rain,
It was pouring down now.

The rain was still pounding,
As my golden coloured friend
Flashed by,
I was very worried.

I had finally reached my destination,
Home was the best place to be,
I was finally here.

This was the best part,
Getting home.

Ross Lagor (11)
Poltair Community School & Sports College, St Austell

The Twister

The pulling, dragging and queuing to the slippery top.
As the Scout boys stare at me with their droopy eyes.
Ouch, ouch, oh no, how heavy, I hate coming down this side.

Their feet pushing in the back of my boating bouncy head.
'Hold on tight!' What does he mean?
I always slip and slop everywhere.
Hang on why are there *beeps*?
The splashing water bouncing back in my face.
Bang, bang, ow! why do I have to come down here?

I'm splashing against the yellow side,
The water helping me wave and shout to the people at the bottom,
We pull and reach to get there.
Finally we are at the bottom
And I am thrown onto the elevator
So someone can ride me next.

Jade Lambert O'Donoghue (11)
Poltair Community School & Sports College, St Austell

Motion

M ovement of a speeding train
O ver bridges *clickety-clack*
T hrough the tunnels black as night
I nto old and dusty stations
O ut again into the light
N ot too far to destination.

Philippa Leaity (11)
Poltair Community School & Sports College, St Austell

Aeroplanes

A eroplanes whoosh and whizz,
  like a bottle of cherry fizz.
E verybody holds tight,
  whilst the plane begins its flight.
R ain spitting like a waterfall,
  spraying its froth over one and all.
O ver the clouds it flew like a bird,
  very loudly it was heard.
P eeping clouds lit up by the sun,
  shining red like fire to everyone.
L ower it goes eager to end the journey
  for me and my friend.
A eroplane slows we are near to the ground,
  watching the houses all around.
N early to the finish line like a sprinting race,
  slower it goes at a tortoise pace.
E ntering the airport having got off the plane,
  watching the faces as it takes off again.

Lauren Ratcliff (13)
Poltair Community School & Sports College, St Austell

Motion

Motion, motion a little devotion
and it's cracked that's a fact,
you can walk, you can run,
you can swim, you can skim a tiny stone,
it's all motion.
You can trot, you can plod,
you can amble and suddenly it's a . . .
shambles. When you're a *child.*

Darren Perks (12)
Poltair Community School & Sports College, St Austell

Lion In Motion

The heartbeat of Africa
beating steadily in the sun
as she crouches silently
waiting for her prey to come

Suddenly a zebra trots by
the lion's heart quickens
as she springs to her feet
and the hunt begins

She swiftly moves across the plains
the zebra panics and quickly runs
the lion's heart pounds faster
as she charges behind

Faster and faster she runs
then leaps rapidly into the air
and brings down the zebra
the chase is over.

Amy Plowman (11)
Poltair Community School & Sports College, St Austell

Motion

The motion in the ocean goes mainly up and down
With fish, whales and sharks tossing and turning
As they go with the current
The motion in the ocean goes mainly round and round
With all the baby fish finding their way around.

Nicholas James Parr (11)
Poltair Community School & Sports College, St Austell

Motion With Horses

Three - two - one
And she's off
With an almighty start
By taking on the first jump

This pony loves to gallop
In-between all the fences
And look how he is
Eating up the ground

Here is the water jump
Splish splash splosh
And over the jump . . .
And gee up

Halfway through the course,
The zigzag jump
Awaits them
And on they go.

This pony is quality
You can see it in his movement,
He must be worth
A fortune.

Heidi Masters (12)
Poltair Community School & Sports College, St Austell

Kangaroos

K angaroos leaping far and wide,
A mazing animals of the outback, moving as quick as quick can be,
N ewborn Joeys resting in Mummy's pouch,
G racious mammals of the bush,
A ustralia main attraction,
R oos or Joeys as they're called
O blivious to all dangers,
O ffended no one, protected by their mummy who's
S pecially known for her strong hind legs and boxing gloves (which
       the strongest punch and the fastest kick are developed).

Rosie Wilson (11)
Poltair Community School & Sports College, St Austell

A Rugby Ball

It is so hard being a rugby ball unless I'm flat,
First they kick me and then they drop me,
Spinning like a roundabout,
Cold hands *eeerrr,*
I'm dropped. *Kick, ouch!* I'm flying.

Splash, eeerrr, wet, cold, sticky mud,
Uh oh, six giants hurling towards me,
Pile on,
Ow! someone with warm hands,
I'm flying, I'm looping, *wheee,*
Big metal poles, am I going to make it? *Ohh, ee,*
Try.

I'm in the middle of the pitch again,
Lots of people,
Argh! Heavyweight,
He's running at the speed of light,
Man on the horizon,
Closing fast.

Bang, crash, fist,
Fight,
Red card,
He he he he! Ha! Ha!
He punched the red,
Kicked the other team.

Threw me at him,
Crack my leather,
I bounced and . . .
Pop
Game over,
Well, for me anyway.

Joshua Nel (11)
Poltair Community School & Sports College, St Austell

Clouds

Swirling, twirling, spinning,
As light as a feather.
Cart wheeling, rolling, jumping,
A bouncy jelly,
Flowing steadily over the world,
Beaches, towns and countryside.

Vibrant and springy,
Always shape-shifting.
Twisting, stretching,
Skating and scooting.
Forever flying
High in the sky.

Flipping, flopping,
Fearlessly flapping.
Airy and carefree,
Fluffy and free.
As innocent as a baby,
As frilly as a flower.

Until huge, slumping, plodding, grey clouds,
Grey with grumpiness,
Scowl as they lurch along.
The white cloud tumbling, fumbling, mumbling,
The white clouds start to merge
Building into a towering mass of white cotton wool

The flying, floating clouds
Sail slowly up, up, up
Until they reach the bright light
Which vanishes them all into thin air!

Katie Ford (12)
Poltair Community School & Sports College, St Austell

Life Without Motion

What would the world be without motion?
No one could move,
Lack of commotion.

No more traffic on the road,
So there's no need to learn,
The Highway Code.

There aren't any aeroplanes that can fly,
Just some clouds,
In the sky.

People can't swim, sway or dance
And because you can't move,
You can't run and prance.

No one could live without motion
You see it's like a magic potion.

Bryony Walker (11)
Poltair Community School & Sports College, St Austell

Traffic

T he traffic moves grumpily
R oads are so bumpy
A nd it feels as if the car has *stopped*
F eeding the birds happily
F rederick Potter sitting beautifully
I' m going to be late for school
C B my tutor group staring at me as I walk in late!

Jade Gardiner (11)
Poltair Community School & Sports College, St Austell

The Cheetah's Foot

I'm still and resting.
    And then, I'm nailed first in the air as
The rest of the body stretches.
    My pad is on the floor as the nose sniffs,
Then I'm thudding slowly, then faster and faster.
    I've stopped . . . still . . .
And I'm off again like a motorbike
    Pounding through the grass like a lawn mower.
Now I'm in the air gliding through the sky.
    I hit something soft, furry, black and white.
What's this? Err, it's wet, it's blood!
    The mouth must be eating, *yuck!*
Yes, I'm walking, I'm going to rest, at last!
    I find my soft patch and the body lies down.
That was hard work, and my nails hurt.
    Now I've got to get lunch.

Louise Haley (11)
Poltair Community School & Sports College, St Austell

The Squirrel

The squirrel flees into the trees
Away from all the thieves
Who steal all his nuts.
He has many cuts upon his face
He leaps around the trees with grace
Towards his nest
Where he will curl up and rest
But then his nest begins to fray
And the squirrel fell out of its dray
He was falling, falling
And hit the ground
Then he found
He was dead!

Joe Higman (12)
Poltair Community School & Sports College, St Austell

The Ride Of My Life

Step by step,
Up through the door,
My heart racing
Like wildfire!
As I take my seat
Looking around,
When my eyes are fixed . . .
Fixed upon the window
We weren't even moving,
But the people looked so small.
I'm up so high,
Yet they are so low down.
I started to shake
When I strapped myself in,
As we started to move
On the runway,
Catching speed
And we're up
Flying up into the clouds.
It felt like a roller coaster
Just speeding upwards,
Going faster and faster,
Until finally we're up
And I can't see the ground.
After about three hours
A speaker gets turned on.
'Ready for landing.'
Steeply heading down,
Bump! We're down!

Sophie Bonney (11)
Poltair Community School & Sports College, St Austell

Pas De Deux

As the music swells
I run across the stage,
gathering speed
before splitting my legs
as I hang in space for a second,
air rushing past my body.

Bright lights blur together
as I turn faster and faster,
fixing my eyes on a neon
exit sign in the black void.

With every step
I feel knives plunging into my toes,
but still I must keep smiling
through the sweat which blinds me.

Then I am in his arms
we move as one,
skin against skin,
spinning unstoppably,
eyes locked together.

Until I must trust him totally,
submit as I am flung into the air,
weightless for a moment,
alone above their heads,
time stands still.

My stomach jolts.
Relief.
He has caught me.

Talei Lakeland (16)
Poltair Community School & Sports College, St Austell

Cat And Mouse

Back hunched, hair stood on end.
Some things just run around the bend,
Quick, quick, you're too slow.
Please, oh please don't let go.
It's running, it's running, ever so fast
Oh no, oh no, you've ran past its house
You can see his shadow in there . . .
Look he's on his way out!
Here we go again past the shed,
Past the dog's bed.
Hang on - where's he gone?
He's got away,
Oh well . . .
There's always another day!

Abigail Whiteman (12)
Poltair Community School & Sports College, St Austell

Tennis

The tennis ball whistled past the net,
Back and forth, back and forth,
Travelling at the speed of light.
The tennis ball's accelerating,
Faster, faster breaking the sound barrier,
The ball's getting hot, hot, hot,
It's going to melt.
The ball whistled past the net where
The man was standing,
He ran, faster than humanly possible,
He returned the ball with venom.
The other man hit it with his hardest hit,
It whistled down the line,
He had won!

Peter Churchill (12)
Poltair Community School & Sports College, St Austell

The Tiger

Alone the tiger prowls around
His head held high
He wanders round his homeland pride
With thoughts of beasts in which he can feed upon.

His eyes do glisten in the sun
Like great blue sapphires
His white neck intimidates those who threaten him
And the camouflage of black and white and oranges
Gives a beautiful feel to this deadly creature.

He edges his home
He steps out his front door
Carefully striding into his kitchen
The antelope are running and the hyenas are laughing free.

The shadows lurk
As the sun drifts down
Where is the tiger? He's gone!
Then a jump and a pounce and a catch.

The tiger smothers his prey with one paw.
He eats happily before prowling back
To his mysterious home.

Holly Julian (12)
Poltair Community School & Sports College, St Austell

The Fastest Car

As the car dodged the traffic
everyone looked as if it was magic
as the car flew through the air
the public could hardly not stare
as the car screeched to a halt
it sounded like he had a loose bolt
as the car sped down the road
he saw a shopper doing Morse code
as the car got pulled over
the police realised he wasn't sober!

Tom Bray (12)
Poltair Community School & Sports College, St Austell

The Art Of Motion

Motion is a physical art
Swirling and spinning, shifting and sliding
Every movement is a ballet
We witness Swan Lake at every step
The Nutcracker is performed with every breath
Yet all this is yet to be noticed.

The starlings' dance of a thousand wings
Writhing and lashing with each turn
The lead appears, falcon diving and delving
Into the heart of the undulating mass
The dancers veer and surge to escape
The ballet ends but no rapturous applause, no red curtain.

The cheetahs' dance of midnight stalking
Sliding and shifting as each paw falls, then
Exploding forth from grassy binds as prey scatter
Undulating and whirling in a maelstrom of life
The prey slow to a stop exchanging grief, one less to their number
The ballet ends but no rapturous applause, no red curtain.

The serpents' dance of coiled ambush
Seething and sliding as each coil unfolds
Darting forth to an unsuspecting flank
A burst of shock as the fangs hit home
The victim falls as animation ebbs from its limbs
The ballet ends but no rapturous applause, no red curtain.

Motion is a physical art
Swirling and spinning, shifting and sliding
Every movement is a ballet
We witness Swan Lake at every step
The Nutcracker is performed with every breath
Now all this can be experienced.

Sam Hicks (13)
Poltair Community School & Sports College, St Austell

The Lion

The lion crept
The lion clawed
The lion pounced
The lion roared
The lion crept onto its prey
Would it kill or eat today?
It missed its victim
The chase began
Through the forest
Covering miles of land
Bounding over old tree trunks
Leaping off of rotten stumps
The lion gave up and
Stopped to drink
It loved to think
Whilst stopping to drink,
It drank and drank . . .
Jumped off the bank
And into the murky water
To cool off.

Kaci Rickard (12)
Poltair Community School & Sports College, St Austell

The Car

The car stalled and skidded,
It skidded to a halt.
The dustbins roared
And the streetlights loomed.
The wind whistled,
Which slapped people in the face.
The lorries groaned
And the car lights glared.
The people carried buses
And the cars stalled and skidded.

Luke Best (12)
Poltair Community School & Sports College, St Austell

The Bird?

It swept over the sea
And around the quay
Where the fisherman fish
For food on their dish

It scours the land
For things to be found
To take to another place
But don't believe it is safe

Over the hills, higher and higher
It watches the people below
It soars over the valleys
Until it is time to lie low.

Rachel Dowrick (13)
Poltair Community School & Sports College, St Austell

Heron

Flies down just like a glider plane,
In sunshine, snow and heavy rain.
He pecks the fish in a flash,
The others jump, flip, *splish and splash!*
Here comes a gardener, 'Get outta here,'
He uses his quick-loyal ear,
One twitch and he is out of sight,
Or turns to give a nasty fright.
He twists around in a second,
By his family he is beckoned.
Off he swoops back to the nest
To have a well-deserved rest.

Sam Armstrong (12)
Poltair Community School & Sports College, St Austell

The Dancer

Starting slowly, a snail's pace,
Floating through the air like a bird,
Leotard as black as the night sky,
Skirt as bright as a diamond's reflection.

Speeding up, a rocket, a Concorde,
Turning and twirling like a spinning top,
Elegantly drifting around the room,
Hardly touching the floor at all.

Tour jetes, pirouettes, entrechats,
One move transforms into another, and another,
Flowing smoothly, continuously,
Never ending, forever moving.

Sarah Masters (14)
Poltair Community School & Sports College, St Austell

The Raven

Like a dart the raven flies,
Like a daemon before your eyes,
Like a minion of the dark,
It attacks like a spark,
Its claws, sharp as sickles,
Its eyes, cool as nickel,
It soars with all its might,
The evil spawn of the night.

Charles Camps (13)
Poltair Community School & Sports College, St Austell

Motionless

I sit here motionless,
Someone help me.
They just pass by,
Not a care in the world.

But they don't just pass,
They stop and stare stupidly.
It's not my fault,
It's only my legs.

They look at me,
As if I have no feelings.
But what do they know?
I'm really not that different.

I want to run around in the playground
And go for a swim in the sea,
I want to dance at the discos
And run a race on sports day.

I want to do things
That the other children do.
But I can't
And it hurts.

Verity Walker (13)
Poltair Community School & Sports College, St Austell

Not Yet

Crying she knows what she left behind,
That thing there always in her mind.
She thinks, *never stop trying, never stop dreaming,*
But it's too late now all there is is screaming.
Now hearing the scream of the wound that needs healing,
She prays it will stop, she keeps on believing
That someone will find it and love it dearly,
Scenes run through her mind but not very clearly.
Running so fast it stings her eyes
But then suddenly to her surprise
The hounds have gone, the horns have died
And now she sits there happy she tried.
Now slinking away back to her set,
She wonders if they've gone, but no not yet . . .

Yasmin Sweet (13)
Poltair Community School & Sports College, St Austell

Running Down The Road

The man ran down the road
In the horrible pouring rain
He skipped, ran, walked, jumped
Suddenly he fell over a bump
He rolled down, around and around
Then he heard a horrible sound
The sound was like something breaking
Something ahead overtaking
It was a car up ahead
Then he found himself in a hospital bed.

Kelly Buscombe (13)
Poltair Community School & Sports College, St Austell

Motion

I started to run slowly at first
I was scared, I thought my brain would burst
I carried on, I felt really cold
I started to run towards the sunset which was gold.

I started to run fast
I thought I would come last
Someone ran past me I felt my tension rise
A girl asked me for my shoe size
I ignored her and kept on running, I slowed down
I was running so slowly I couldn't see town

I started to speed up
I saw a dog which looked like a pup
I heard screaming, I turned around, I screamed
It was the most awful sight I had ever seen

A girl fell flat on her face
There was blood everywhere
Everyone stopped and stared
I didn't know what to do, I felt sick

The ambulance came, I heard sirens
The girl got rushed to hospital
The race still went on
I was the only one running
I didn't know where everyone else had gone

It felt like a dream
I felt really ill, I began to scream
There was no one around or any sound
I felt like fainting, I felt funny

I was still running and so was everyone else
There was no blood anywhere
I won the race and it was all just a dream.

Emily Ratcliff (14)
Poltair Community School & Sports College, St Austell

Motion Movement

M oving from place to place,
O ut of one place into another,
T oo many ways to travel,
I can never decide,
O n days like today pollution is everywhere,
N ow everything is dying.

M otion,
O cean,
V ariation,
E nough motion on this land,
M any ways to travel in transport,
E nd of motion,
N othing moves,
T oo many ways of motion.

Lauren Blazier (11)
Poltair Community School & Sports College, St Austell

Motion

Swooped through the air,
Thinking life isn't fair,
Looking down at the ground,
Sensing the movement around.

Tap! Tap! Feeling the vibration,
Moving around,
Sights its target,
Flies down, close to the ground.

A bird of prey,
Hits the floor,
Clenches to something grey,
A meal at last for its young.

Luke Payne (13)
Poltair Community School & Sports College, St Austell

Motion Is . . .

Motion is everything
Everything is motion
From the slither of a silk green snake
To the beat of a pumping heart.

The turn of a page, to the swimming of
A fish in the deep blue sea
From the leaves blowing in the wind
To the slam of a door.

The fluent motion of a pen
To the blinking of an eye,
From the gushing of water
To the swish of a sword.

The drop of a pin to the trot of a horse
From the speed of a train
To the turn of a wheel.

Motion is everything
Everything is motion.

Megan O'Connell (13)
Poltair Community School & Sports College, St Austell

My Hamster

Her sleek, brown fur,
Becomes a blur,
As she zooms across the floor.
I've tried with all my might,
I've chased her through the night.
She's behind the bookcase now
And there she will stay,
For the rest of the day,
Until I find a way to catch her.

Jade Bradley (12)
Poltair Community School & Sports College, St Austell

Flying High

At the foot of the mountain
I gaze in awe
The dream of the peak
I'll get there I'm sure

Like an ant to a molehill
A fish to a pier
A fox to a giant
A mouse to a deer

It may be long
It may be tough
But I will do it
I'm strong enough

Silently slipping
On step after step
Snowflakes are falling
'Are we nearly there yet?'

I'm halfway there,
5,000 feet high,
As high as a cloud
In the clear blue sky

My joints are tiring
Every step I take
There's a yeti nearby
But I long for a break

At the top I'm higher
Than a hot air balloon
I feel like a bird
On top of the world.

Andora Perkins (13)
Poltair Community School & Sports College, St Austell

Or(!)

Like a fish from a hook I scatter from the shoreline,
Like a lifeless duck I float on the spray of the sea,
Like a weary whale I drift over the whispering waves,
As the ripples of the ocean rise they grow like tall trees into the skies.
I start high-climbing, up, up, up.
Then I soar back down as elegantly as an eagle, with an awkward
broken wing.

Shrill and sharp shriek,
The wind got stronger causing me to tumble like the clothes in
a washing machine.
Salt water squirting and spurting,
The movement was making me seasick as if on a boat that rocks me
from side to side.
Swoosh, swish, splash,
The water had soaked all through the wooden splinters of my skin
like a sopping sponge.

Like an ant I keep crawling back up the rolling mountains,
Like a snake in the grass the sea hisses with the venom of alarm,
Like a kangaroo I bounce on the waves with springs
As the mist creeps in like a jaguar in prey,
I chase the waves like a dog with a cat.
Then I hop away as a rabbit would from a hunter with a gun.

The water is an ice-cold shower, fresh from the seashore.
From the sky I see a line of lightning flying through the air,
The charcoal clouds have started grumbling and growling like a tiger
rolling on the hills.
I see a flickering glimpse of light reflecting in the swaying waves.
The splattering of water has calmed to a mere ripple,
The ripple to such a stillness I still rock and spin.

Like the pounding of an elephant jumping up in joy,
Like the roar of a lion in a chase for food,
Like the screech of a piglet struggling to be free.
As the rumbling turns to a murmur the sea creatures
continue swimming.
I have only one problem: I'm a paddle with a hole!
Then I sink!

Hannah Nel (14)
Poltair Community School & Sports College, St Austell

The Motion Of Words

Words can have their own unique motion,
Different beats and different rhymes,
The words you read form left to right,
The page you read, you progress down.

The genre has an effect too,
Rolling on an endless sea,
Swaying like a ship in a storm
And flying like a careless bird.

Words can be used in many ways,
A speech written by a politician,
A song that stirs your calmed soul,
Sometimes a threat or curse.

So when you read these words just think,
Just how the motion works,
You'll be surprised at what you see,
Like the movement in this verse.

Joseph Green (13)
Poltair Community School & Sports College, St Austell

The Weather's Right

The clouds are running across the sky
they run around the world so high
the movement is slow or fast
it all depends on the forecast

The sun is happy standing still
it will move at its will
the sun is baking hot
your skin is burnt,
it looks like it has rot

The wind is blowing across the world
it turns around as if it has curled
the wind is blowing with all its might
it has no hesitation to put up a fight.

David Blount (13)
Poltair Community School & Sports College, St Austell

Lost!

I'm lost in a place this is hell,
I feel like a prisoner in a cell.

As darkness draws near shadows appear
As day turns into night,
I'm standing here frozen with fear
Like a rabbit at the glare of a light.

As an owl swoops down from its tree,
The raindrops trickle down on me.

The wind is strong and howling
Like a wolf on a full moon
And night creatures are prowling
Like spiders in my room.

I lie here scared and all alone
And I'm startled by a high-pitched tone.

Yellow eyes looking at me
Like cats' eyes on the road,
I hear noises from a tree
Like the croak of a big toad.

Don't know what time it is must be getting late,
I don't think I am ever going to be found at this rate.

Owls hooting in their trees
Like sirens in the night,
In their little families
But some of them take flight.

The beginning of another day
What else can I say?

The sun is shining really bright
Animals running around,
Shining on me like a torch
Whilst I'm lying on the ground.

Emma Thomas (13)
Poltair Community School & Sports College, St Austell

Motion

A photo on the wall catches my eye.
A young woman on a wonderful dappled pony.
The wind whistles through my hair like pan pipes.
I smell the fresh dew from sunrise
As we pass the bluebells on untouched morning grass
Like an explorer taking her first steps on untouched land.

From a black and white print, a little girl laughs.
I scream with delight as the strong but gentle hands of my papa
Send me soaring to the sky on my swing.
My legs kick wildly with excitement
Like a clockwork doll that has burst out of control
The clouds are beckoning me as I fall back to Earth.

A dress is hanging on the door,
Its colours flowing and melting into one another like the ocean.
The whirr of the machine comforts me as night draws in.
My stiff cold hands continue to feed the magic material under
                                                    the needle
Like a sheepdog guiding his sheep into the pen.
My fingers don't stop until dawn.

Next to my head is Jammy, the teddy bear.
The warm glow of Christmas fills our living room.
My beautiful child clambers on my lap with an oddly wrapped present
It is for me.
I carefully unwrap my gift - a teddy bear - 'He's called Jammy,'
                                                    I am told.
I thank my beautiful child, and hug and kiss her.

I can no longer ride, I cannot even walk.
I cannot swing, nor can I push someone on a swing.
My fingers are clenched into unmoveable fists.
I am never again allowed the pleasure of hugging or kissing my child.
I speak only in groans and grunts.
My body is dead, my mind alive - I am confined within myself.

Ella West (13)
Poltair Community School & Sports College, St Austell

What Can You See?

Have you ever been able to look up and up and up,
till your neck hurts?
I have.

If you look high, you will see swallows.
They perform their own dance, flight and rhythmical patterns
that twist and sway in the summer breezes.

If you look higher, you will see clouds.
thin and wispy or plump and cuddly.
They toss and turn playing hide-and-seek in and out of the sunlight,
casting shadows that slide and drift across fields of corn.

If you look higher, you will see fairies.
Chasing, searching for pots of endless gold and happiness
at the bottom of multicoloured rainbows.

If you look higher, you will see dreams.
Changing, contrasting and growing.
Flowing like musical notes from an orchestra
or seeping into the ether layer of freedom and prosperity
to all of mankind.

If you look higher, you will see no more.
Life ends and the new unknown begins.

Does it hurt yet?

Ysella Wood (13)
Poltair Community School & Sports College, St Austell

She Lay There Motionless

She lay there motionless
In excruciating pain
Waiting for her puppies to arrive
The hours seemed like days

The time has come
They're here
Three little puppies
What sacred creatures

They lie there
Blind as bats
Like in a distressed coma
Dead to the world

At two weeks
They take their first step
What a precious moment
Which I will cherish forever.

Kirsty Kent (13)
Poltair Community School & Sports College, St Austell

Waves

All is calm on a summer's morning
as the sun begins to rise.
Later the waves start to grow,
slapping the shore creating a new picture.
White horses come out and crash down
stealing sandcastles on the way.
The storm clouds appear,
the rain is near;
the waves begin to dance.
All is calm on a summer's morning
as the sun begins to rise.
Later the waves begin to grow,
slapping the shore, creating a new picture.

Lauren Beard (12)
Poltair Community School & Sports College, St Austell

Gothic Gal

You live your life in darkness,
in agony and in pain,
you decide to dress in black,
that's something you always gain.
You look like someone from down below,
you look so fast, yet move so slow,
you are really cool to know.
You look like you're upset,
although you wander around happily,
you don't dress in colours only black and grey.
You live your life in darkness,
in agony and in pain,
hopefully you'll read this,
so I don't have to write it again.

Michaela Dyer (13)
Poltair Community School & Sports College, St Austell

Moving From Home

I wish my dad was here
he would help us through
not that nasty man who made us move.

Things were going fine till he came.
He was pure evil,
he took my life away.

I would stand there and watch him change.
One minute he was fine,
the next minute he was like an animal
on the hunt to kill.

Bobbie Musgrave (13)
Poltair Community School & Sports College, St Austell

Motion

I'm dying down now
It's been a long day
The trees are asleep
Hooray! Hooray!

In the morning when I blow
Curtains swish, papers scatter
In the evening when I blow
Gates creak, dustbins clatter.

Now it's quiet I'll blow the corn
You might hear it whisper softly on the lawn
It's getting dark, windows rattle
I wonder if I've won my battle.

Jasmin Hicks (13)
Poltair Community School & Sports College, St Austell

What Am I Looking At?

I was lying on my bed
reading my magazine.
Oh no, what was that?
Is it my cat?
No! No!
Is it a rat?
So I crept towards the door
I opened it slowly.
I crept around the door
I'm getting closer
it's only the toaster!

Samantha Voysey (13)
Poltair Community School & Sports College, St Austell

Them!

I sit down on my bed
I look at the gap in the door
I see it
I see it
It's there
It's coming
I hide in my bed shaking in terror
It pulls back the covers slowly
It's there staring at me with green eyes
Its breath smells like liver
It opens its mouth and saliva drips
My sister Azaria comes in
I see her green eyes
Oh no! She's one of them!
She hit it
She says, 'Run!'
So I do
Azaria says, 'Follow me.'
So I do
Oh my god she's tricked me
My mum and dad are gone
They are like them too
I sing a song that is sad
Azaria vanishes into thin air
Once again I live
Or do I?

Amanda Hicks (14)
Poltair Community School & Sports College, St Austell

Movement In Animals

Movement, a word,
Yet has so many meanings.
The movement of a bird,
The simple up and up, flap and flap,
The jerky movement of some birds
Compared to the silken, fluid motion
Of a flock of starlings,
To the quickness of a falcon diving down.

The movement of a hare,
The swiftness of a young buck hare,
To the old hare loping across the field,
Like a wounded deer,
Yet he still avoids the hunter and predator.

The movement of an elephant,
The slow, ponderous wandering of adult and calf,
To the thundering stampede of the herd,
Which is startling to even the elephants themselves.
Movement.

The movement of a fish,
The relative slowness of a whale,
Then the lightning quick reactions of a barracuda,
The slow death swim of a shark
And the mass movement of cod.

Christopher Stanlake (13)
Poltair Community School & Sports College, St Austell

Taxi

Walking out, the air fills my lungs,
Looking round I see the lights,
The taxi's coming closer.
I stick my hand out, feeling vulnerable
Like I'm a beggar.
It pulls over, I get in.

'Where to please?'
'Town centre thanks!'
The car moves and my body jolts as a shock.
I can just about find where the handle is
And I wind the window down.

A gust of wind hits past my face
And my breath is stolen.
Quickly moving on, everything passes me
Like a picture show.
The faces of people passing
Makes me wonder of life outside my own.

A big red light comes closer - traffic lights.
We stop but one minute feels like an hour.
Watching cars pass, seeing all the people move.
Who are they? Feels like I know them.
Green! We move! Gradually we get slower.
'Town centre!'
I step out and pay the driver,
'Cheers mate!'
I start walking on, but then I suddenly stop.
'Where am I going?'

Jenny Siu (14)
Poltair Community School & Sports College, St Austell

Superman

Once Superman
Now a prisoner of Mother Nature
Just laying there or sitting in a chair,
Motionless, motionless.

One day a finger
Twitches, twitches.
He moves! He moves!
'A miracle!' they cry.

A finger, a hand, an arm,
One by one, he moves.
Again, again, he moves.
To water they go.

Aided by many, he takes his first step.
He steps, he walks, again, again,
He moves! He moves!

It's on the news,
It's in the papers.
He moves! He moves!
'A miracle!' they cry.

Soon he may do it
He could walk
Maybe even fly.
Who knows what will happen
Maybe he will be
Our Superman once more.

Charly Scott (13)
Poltair Community School & Sports College, St Austell

Wind

Leaves fall, grass sways, relieved sighs,
The breeze as cool as an empty, lonely fridge.
A hurricane to an ant, yet a breeze to us humans.
Whoosh! A time of refreshment, a breath from the distance.
Never ending . . . perpetual.
Plains of consistent grass, wavering.
Each blade a soldier marching vigorously,
Yet going nowhere.
What be the reason of wind, where did it come from?
Ambiguous questions with different answers,
Never soon to be answered. No one knows.

Mark Miles (13)
Poltair Community School & Sports College, St Austell

Frog Or Prince

Is he a frog or maybe a prince?
The confusion really makes him wince.
Find the answer, help him with this,
Be the one to give him a kiss.
Be his princess,
He'll clean up all of your mess.
He'll buy you a bear,
So you'd better beware.
In late fall, as wind gusts blow,
Your bear hibernates before the snow.
In early spring, sweet scent of a flower,
Your new tiger wakes as he feels a light shower.
Through jungle shadows your tiger will prowl,
Just don't be afraid, sometimes he'll growl.
He's not fierce, so don't run away,
Now you're all the best of friends and you'll play all day.

Sarah Huxham (12)
Teign School, Kingsteignton

Maria And Stefano

Their first encounter was at the dock,
She met him at the grandfather clock.
Her heart melted with warmth from his glowing charm,
She longed for comfort in his arms.
Captain called, 'All aboard,' with might,
Then the man said to her, 'Tomorrow night!
As twilight falls like clouds of ink,
we'll meet again, in arms we'll sink!'

She sighed and waved as he sailed away,
On the battleship, so far away.
She skipped home, anticipation deep inside,
Her love was the thing she dared not hide.
She entered her home and yearned for his face,
His love for her, his sweet embrace.
Crying in pain he knelt on the ship,
An unfair victim of the whip.
He'd refused to kill an elderly man,
now he dreamed of tomorrow, his girl on the sand.

He begged for mercy, but at that time,
the gun was shot, his end was nigh.
The last thought he had as the agony spread,
was how he'd ever see her face again, now he's dead.
The world disappeared as his heart let go,
her sweet touch he'd never know.

Meanwhile, Maria had no clue,
as she slept in her bed in sheets of blue.
The next day, it just seemed so long
and she leapt with glee when twilight had come.
She put on her dress, the finest she had,
she had to look her best for this lad!
She ran to the beach, with tears of joy,
the time had come, she'd see this boy.

Again, they'd be two lovers in bloom,
their laughter and love could never spell doom.
But his friend she'd seen at the dock that day,
had brought bad news Maria's way.

As he cried himself, and let her know,
she'd lost her darling Stefano.
It felt like her heart had been pierced with a knife,
how could she go on without him in her life?

She'd barely known him a minute, but was first to believe,
he was her true love, so her heart he'd receive.
She ran to the cliffs and cried to the sea,
'There is still a way you can be with me!'
She was still for a second, to catch her breath,
then with no hesitation, she leapt to her death.

So she'd given her life, to be with her love
and higher than anywhere, way up above,
their spirits joined together, and Maria was right,
their destiny did lie in the air that night.

Carla Julier (13)
Teign School, Kingsteignton

The Siberian Tiger

The black and yellow hunter seeks his prey,
Silent and sleek in the moonlight,
Prowling, glistening teeth bared,
Ready, still with jagged fur.

Through the reeds like a dash of wind,
He encounters a spot of blood
Lifts his nose and lets out a cry,
For he has found his lunch.

As stealthy as a jackal,
He defends his pride and joy
He licks the world as clean as a plate,
Because danger is everywhere.

He stalks off, lips curled,
He knows he rules the jungle
Hesitating, ears pricked like brittle thorns,
Quietly he slips off to sleep.

Natalie Chivers (12)
Teign School, Kingsteignton

Upset In The Urban

A new day is dawning,
A new body floating in the canal,
A new corpse in the mortician's surgery,
Cops and robbers head it off,
Pistols at dawn now,
Bullets crack,
The detective, he ain't ever lookin' back,
The battlefields of Central Park,
The slaughterhouse of Trafalgar Square,
Gunshots in Beverly Hills,
Next of kin in mourning,
Death at the Eiffel Tower,
Murder at the Reichstag,
More dead in the cemeteries,
Insane in the nuthouse,
Wounded in the casualty,
Pain-stricken in the police station.

Nuclear holocaust, bullets flaring now
The great axe of life,
The men in the gutter,
The women in the gun shop,
The kids in the help-homes,
The gun-toting murderers,
The scamming millionaires,
The knife in the dark alley,
The shady with the cocaine,
Obituaries, funerals, deaths and thievery,
The vice's iron fingers are becoming buttery,
Politics in despair,
The president a headless chicken,
Corrupt cops, slavery and mutilation,
Car thefts, harassing and assassination.

Devon Tucker (11)
Teign School, Kingsteignton

I Wanna Be Yours

Let me be your ruler
And I'll be straight with you
Let me be your computer
And I'll always help you
Let me be your imaginary friend
Our friendship will never end
And I'll always be there
I wanna be yours.

Let me be your TV
You can keep me on forever
Let me be your DVD
Play me like a cat and feather
Let me be your hairbrush
I will make your hair look lush
With hair bands and bows.

Let me be your garden bench
For you to lay and rest your head
Let me be your garden fence
And protect you sleeping in your bed
Let me be your night light
So I can see you shining bright
My love for you will be as long
As the time humans live on Earth
Years, years, years, years and years
I love you and
I wanna be yours.

Craig Field (11)
Teign School, Kingsteignton

So What? Do Bullies Care?

So what if she was strange?
So what if you can make her cry?
You're the tough man.
Go on, push her around
She can't fight back.

Who's the big man? You.
So what if she's crying?
So what if she's bleeding?
This is fun
Go on let her run this time
This time she's lucky.

You'll always have the upper hand
So what if she comes to school tomorrow prepared?
So what if she has a knife?
You can beat her down
Go on, go into the bathroom
Go open the cubicle door.

You were the first one to find her.
Guess what? She has blood on her wrists.
Guess what? She's left a note.
What makes you think you have the right
To harm someone so badly?
You killed her.
So what if no one speaks to you?
So what if no one can even look at you?
So what?

Kerenza Flanary (11)
Teign School, Kingsteignton

I Want To Be Yours

Let me be your radio
I will talk to you every day
Let me be your hairbrush
I will stop your hair from fray
Let me be your pocket
So you will always have money
Let me be your TV
So you can watch something funny
I wanna be yours.

Let me be your legs
So I can keep you upright
Let me be your bodyguard
So I can fight your fights
Let me be your lights
So you can turn me on
Let me be your fire alarm
So I can keep you safe
I wanna be yours.

Philip Houdmont (11)
Teign School, Kingsteignton

The Kaleidoscope Sky

When I look at the sky,
I see rainbow colours,
Seven beautiful ones.
Suddenly -
The wind blows all the clouds,
Shapes appear and change.
They're cartoons, people, things . . .
And then when it's evening,
It shows uncountable colours in the sky.
So pretty.
If you don't believe me,
You can look up at the sky now
And see how it changes.

Iris Chan (12)
The Bolitho School, Penzance

Watery Hell

Plop!
I gently float down and quietly settle on the soft, velvet river
Hardly making a sound

Slowly and calmly
Pulled down river

Acceleration suddenly
Like a lion breaking into a chase

Moments later
Caught between the rage of rushing water
And the proud rocks.

Water nudges,
Pushes me, with such power!

Thrust into the air
Viciously

Falling
Falling

I look down

Fear caresses me
The wind swirls me
Slow my fall!

Paralysed
By what lies beneath
Waiting

Waiting to drag me under
To the watery hell below . . .

Phoebe Quinn (14)
The Bolitho School, Penzance

I Think School Is Number One

School is great,
With my mate.

We run around,
We make a sound.

Break is fun,
We eat a bun.

I think school is number one!

Always dashing to and fro,
Always, always on the go.

English is great!
It's maths I hate!

I think school is really cool.

Homework's bad,
Makes me mad.

My friends are ace,
We like to race.

Sport is fun
In the sun.

I think school is number one!

Megan Halford (11)
The Bolitho School, Penzance

Clowns

Clowns are bouncy,
They dance all over the place.
Clowns are larger than life,
They always put a smile on your face.
Clowns make you laugh
All day long,
And with their painted smiles,
They can do no wrong.

Chelsea Jelbert (11)
The Bolitho School, Penzance

Fish

Fish are in a shoal
And they are not very bright.
And when they see a shark,
They swim out of sight.

They always see the dolphin
Jumping in and out,
They're very, very ugly,
So when you see one, shout!

They're very strange creatures,
They're quite amazing too,
Breathing under water,
Even when they need the loo!

Georga Longhurst (11)
The Bolitho School, Penzance

School

I love school, it's really fun,
Especially when all my work gets done!

Then I go out to play,
The best part of the day.

My friends are so great,
To argue with them, I hate.

Homework, homework is the worst,
I like punctuation and verse!

Amie Hembrough (11)
The Bolitho School, Penzance

The Limey

There once was a little green lime
Who engaged in a lifetime of crime
Though a master of stealing,
His own dodgy dealing
And profits concealing,
Led his gang of fruit
To give him the boot
And purloin his loot.

In a damp prison camp
Like a broken old tramp,
Lime crouched by his lamp
And shivered with cramp.

That lamp burnt the camp.

So ending his life of crime,
Lime decided to turn to rhyme,
Scratching out verse after verse in the grime
But failed time, after time, after time,
Then having a go at mime,
He earned the occasional dime.

One day grabbing a bucket of slime
Lime swiftly started to climb
Coating the town in black brine,
He eventually ran out of time,
As the clock struck its midnight chime.

Calum Humphreys (11)
The Bolitho School, Penzance

Traffic

Horns parping,
Headache arrives,
M5,
A million cars and me.
Seven mile an hour
Slow
Slower
Even slower
Stop
Dead
Five hours have passed
Still here
Ambulance rushes
Police too
And firemen troop behind.
Moving again!

Philippa Hemsworth (12)
The Bolitho School, Penzance

My Life Sucks!

My life sucks!
I never get to see my dad.
When I go to bed at night
I think how my life will turn out.
In the morning when I wake up,
I wonder what will happen
In the world today.
When I am asleep, I wonder
If my life could get any worse.

Katie Robinson (11)
The Bolitho School, Penzance

Sandy Beaches

I see the sea rushing up the shore.
Pebble chase!

I hear people laughing and playing,
Parents chat.

I tread on the sand, barefoot,
Avoiding the hot patches.

I feel the warm sun burning my back.
Breeze on my face.

I see the blue sky,
Clouds roll on.

I see sandals deserted.
Their owners are swimming.

I hear the surfers on the waves,
Laughing, chatting, giggling!

Katie Woodstock (12)
The Bolitho School, Penzance

Stone

The stone sat on the beach,
Like a little leech.
A boy comes along
And throws it in - with a pair of tongs!
The stone,
Now alone.
A fish swam by -
Then the same boy, with a gun
Did what he did, for fun
The fish,
Now dead.

Andrew Cocking (12)
The Bolitho School, Penzance

River Drifting

Sun blazing down,
Water reflecting.
Peaceful sitting by the river,
Slow
Current.
I'll go for a swim
Walk upstream,
Lie back,
Let the current take me
Downstream.
Relaxing, drifting.
Smooth, drifting,
No more being weightless,
I'll walk upstream again.
Slippery and slimy stones under my feet.
Splashing as I fall,
Leaving the peaceful river to itself.

Sarah Williams (11)
The Bolitho School, Penzance

Beaches

The hot sand fries your feet.
The bitter sea bashing
Against the rough rocks.
Divers diving into the refreshing sea.
Children playing and making sandcastles,
The boiling sun,
Burning our faces.

Emily Bowser (12)
The Bolitho School, Penzance

The Drifting Leaf

I am a leaf, rushing down,
A river flowing below me.
I see the rocky bottom below the sparkling water.
Green, blurred leaves around me.

I am a small, elegant leaf,
Body of deep dark green
Attached to this grand oak.

My brothers, sisters and friends
Have fallen onto the river.
Whooshing past day and night.

I have fallen and I rush past.
Away from my oak forever.
'Where am I going?' I shout.

I am lonely,
I am scared,
I wish and hope that I find my grand oak
And return.

The rains start pushing me
To the sharp, rocky bottom of the river.

That night I still flow down the river.
The stars dance happily,
The moon smiles
And I lie here lonely,
Unwanted,
Uncared for.
I am a leaf.
I will be alone now.
I will rot and wilt alone.

Amber Davey (11)
The Bolitho School, Penzance

Love

Love is a journey
You never know what's round the corner
Could be good
Could be bad
It could make you happy
It could make you sad
Then when you go round that corner
And you see what lies ahead
You know you should face it head on
But you can't remember what you said

You pass that first hurdle
And go smooth for a while
But then hills make you tired
And you feel you can't go on
You tell yourself to keep going
You try
You try again
The other says it won't work out
Cos at some point 'we're gonna fail'

But you struggle on
Love pushes you on
And you get over that hill
And you go straight for a while
You want love never to end
You want it to go on and on
And on and on
But you never know what's next
What will be around the bend
Round that corner
What will life send?

Laura Nicholas (13)
The Bolitho School, Penzance

My Little Connemara

As his legs land, the mud
Sprays up his elegant legs

We move towards the next jump,
It feels like we are flying
As we gallop across the sun-kissed grass.

He raises his head in
Anticipation of the jump ahead.

The crescendo of his hooves
Fills my head, with electrifying rhythm.

As he prances across the finish line
To the sound of
Cheers all around

I pat his neck
He turns his head
Oh how I love my little Conna.

Suzie Beuttell (13)
The Bolitho School, Penzance

A Smile

Smile in the corner
Coming from nowhere
A quiver
A flutter
A quick flit of laughter
Makes everyone happy.

Holly Monger (14)
The Bolitho School, Penzance

Are You Sure It's Christmas?

Up goes the tinsel,
But it doesn't feel like Christmas.
Up go the holly and the mistletoe,
But it doesn't feel like Christmas.
Mum's making special biscuits,
But it doesn't feel like Christmas.
Friends are coming over,
But it doesn't feel like Christmas.
Mum's putting up the tree,
Dad's putting up the lights,
But it doesn't feel like Christmas.
Bang!
Dad blows the fuses.
Now I know it's Christmas.

Rewan Taylor (12)
The Bolitho School, Penzance

Autumn

Summer's ended
Autumn's begun
Blazing trees around everyone
People laughing and having fun
Hallowe'en is not far to come.

Leaves fall from every branch
The wind joins in the game and dance
Autumn will be ending soon
Leaves drop and sigh
Christmas is coming soon
See you next year I say
Packing up my things
And collecting my sleigh.

Georgia Gillam (112)
The Bolitho School, Penzance

Pencil

Descending onto the paper,
Sliding quickly along its flesh,
Creating markings on the victim's body,
Dashing up and down,
Page after page it blackens,
But its death is near,
For when the pencil lead runs out,
Its head withers
And when its other limbs
Fall off,
They drop
And drop
Until they hit the bottom
Of the bin.

James Waldie (11)
The Bolitho School, Penzance

Dark Cloaks

When light fades,
The dark enters like a play ending.
Strange shapes come to people's minds,
As they gaze into it.
The stars are like small diamonds,
Sewn in.
The moon shines like an unearthly light,
The only hole in the cloak.
Light fades,
An unknown spirit casts his cloak.

Wyatt Phipps (11)
The Bolitho School, Penzance

The Old Man Tree

Down by the river
A tree,
Old but alert,
Like an old man, just waking.
His heavy body grew from the mossy bank.
The body was gnarled,
Grey-brown in colour,
And branches, old and grey,
As wispy hair.
However . . .
Lower branches covered
Lichen - spiky and rough,
As an old man's beard.
The stream ran over his supine trunk,
A blanket, rippling over him.

Chloe Twose (11)
The Bolitho School, Penzance

Waves

The wild wet and salty swell
Slapped over the curved bow of the boat.
White horses sprayed in my face, drenching me.
One minute almost vertical up in the wave!
Then vertical straight down!
The huge, triangular-shaped sail almost touching water,
The wind howling in my ears,
The tiller pulled towards me,
Onto a reach heading home,
Racing to beat the storm!

Josh Barrow (11)
The Bolitho School, Penzance

The Lost Shoe

A shoe is happy in its pair,
They're useful, helpful and serviceable,
But suppose the left shoe is without the right,
They become useless, helpless and worthless.
A trainer would have no one to run with,
A skate shoe would have no one to skate with,
A wellie would have no one to splash with,
A snow-boot would have no one to ski with,
A horseshoe would have no one to trot with.
The shoe is forgotten and no one cares anymore.
Money is spent on a new pair,
And then . . .
The left is back with the right.

Benjamin Biss (11)
The Bolitho School, Penzance

Down To Earth

The day was crisp and bitter.
A frosty hand grasped my throat
And snatched my breath away.
A myriad of pure white crystals
Sifting through the sky
Landing softly on the ground
Waiting silently, to die.

Tazzy Walton (11)
The Bolitho School, Penzance

Shark

His open mouth
Coming,
His sharp skin through the water,
Cutting,
Fin as sharp as a knife,
Teeth like saws.

Bang!

Into my heroes . . .
The metal bars.
With a wave of water into my face -
His powerful tail fins,
And he's off into the dark blue depths.

Alex Weary (13)
The Bolitho School, Penzance

Urban Amazon

The canopy of skyscrapers etch their shape
Into the sky.
Cars scuttle along the ground
Like an army of ants marching
In orderly rows.

Street lamps like rigid, stationary bamboo
Shoot up.

Billy Lane (13)
The Bolitho School, Penzance

Streamline Surfing

Here it comes,
The perfect wave,
First of the set.
Surfers sprinting to the sea,
But most are too late,
Yet I and a few others ride the roller coaster of the sea.

I'm up,
The wave is breaking.
It breaks,
I fly down the barrel.
Surfboards shooting out of the wave,
But not mine.

I ride on.

Alex Sinclair-Lack (12)
The Bolitho School, Penzance

Cheetah

The cheetah's eyes, fixed on its prey,
Behind the pampas,
Hiding.

Deer eat awkwardly,
Big Brother watching,
Perhaps.

The cheetah jumps,
The deer jumps,
Sprinting! Sprinting away!

Zooming in.
A close up.
First prize.

Rebecca White (13)
The Bolitho School, Penzance

A Field Of Horses

The lane calls me to the field
As my beauty greets.
Her velvet muzzle touches me
The apple was gone.

The swish of her long white mane,
The glimpse of her glassy eyes,
As friends call her
Under the apple tree.

The stallion approaches,
His eyes meet my starry gaze.
The walk seems hours.
The herd stares. Still.

Closer, closer, then gallops away.

A gallop as fast as the wind,
As fast as an eagle,
As fast as a spirit in the air.
To me he is a magical horse.

Months pass, with not sight or sound.
My beauty and spirit. Nowhere.
Just then -
A tug, to my surprise . . .

A black foal. So beautiful.

Lucy Bowden (13)
The Bolitho School, Penzance

Underwater

The fish are moving like the sea
Like people on the beach.
The diver swimming around.
Ice creams are bought for a pound.
Poor fish are getting shot,
A rock is bashed about by the sea.
People run in, hitting the waves.

Patrick Bone (12)
The Bolitho School, Penzance

The Sniper

Crack! The trigger is pulled. The bullet flies.
People drop to the floor and pray nobody dies.
But the target is hit.

The sniper lies still,
Quite pleased with his kill.
He hopes he's not been spotted.

As panic ensues, people shout and scream,
Though the body has not yet been seen.
It lies cold and motionless.

Lying there drenched in blood,
The body lies still in the mud,
Because of an evil, twisted man.

In just a few seconds a life is taken,
All because of religion.
Cold-blooded killing is not the answer to our problems.

Nick Robinson (14)
The Bolitho School, Penzance

The Sports Car

A sports car
Black as the night
Slick as water
The engine purrs like a panther
Speeding away
Like a lion to its prey
Reaching its destination.

Danyal Drew (12)
The Bolitho School, Penzance

Corruption

Corruption all around us
The sick and the poor

The families are hungry
Always needing more

People on the streets
Every day, at least one we meet

People begging
And people pleading

Sorrow and anger
Suffering and beating

Wealthy countries take advantage

Will we live to see another day?
All we can do is hope and pray

Desperation for life. But who can we trust
When there's so much negativity in the world around us?

Money issues
And people crying

What's wrong with the world?
Why are so many dying?

The build up of chemical masses
Suffocation from so many gases

The killing and destroying
All of this we try avoiding

But where can we go?
What can we do?
What's our life worth to you?

Stacey Wall (14)
The Bolitho School, Penzance

My Crush

Life stops
Stops completely, just for a couple of seconds.

Everything,
Everything pauses for just a while
When he looks my way.

My heartbeats jolt,
Jolt out of time.

A curse,
A merciless curse
He holds upon me.

But the curse is no bad curse,
It is a wind, gently moving my heart
Like an autumn leaf.

I feel as though that wind is blowing
Through long strands of glass.

Then is yes,
His pure, gentle, humane eyes
Hit mine -

I freeze.

Georgia Ansell (14)
The Bolitho School, Penzance

Brm Brm!

The motorbike sprints along the road
Like the gazelle across the plain.
The paintwork gleams
Like the sun's rays hitting a mirror.
It races the wind
Like the grand golden eagle.
When it pulls away, it leaves a plume of smoke,
A squid's explosion of ink!
Until it gets home.

John Slater (12)
The Bolitho School, Penzance

Bullet

You are a bullet
Shot out of a gun.
You are a bullet,
A baby, pushed out by your mum.
You are a bullet
Whizzing through the sky,
You are a bullet
And suddenly they die.

You are a bullet
Shot out of a gun.
You are a bullet
In control, job done.
You are a bullet
Flying, no delay.
You are a bullet
And she gets in the way.

You are a bullet
Lying in a pool of blood.
You are a bullet
To be removed from the mud.
You are a bullet
What will happen, now must.
You're a bullet?
Now left to rust.

Sam Reeves (14)
The Bolitho School, Penzance